Global Pay

CW00733908

And the Fintech Changing the Industry

CAROL COYE BENSON

FIRST EDITION

The answers you need about global payments:

How do national payments systems work?
Who are the players in each country?
How do cross-border payments work?
How is interoperability achieved?
What are the fintech providers?
How have they shaped payments innovation?
What is financial inclusion?

GLENBROOK PAYMENTS EDUCATION

This book is part of Glenbrook Partners' Payments Education Program:
a series of workshops, books, articles, webinars and research reports
for payments professionals. The program includes Glenbrook's popular
Payments Boot Camp®, which has been attended by over 24,000 payments
professionals since 2005.

GLENBROOK PRESS

First edition (print only): ISBN 978-0-9827897-6-6
Kindle edition: ISBN 978-0-9827897-7-3

About the Author

 Carol Coye Benson is a founding partner of Glenbrook and an internationally recognized payments expert. Carol created Glenbrook's Payments Education Program, which has educated over 24,000 payments professionals worldwide since its inception. Carol is coauthor of *Payments Systems in the U.S.* which is now in its third edition.

Before founding Glenbrook, Carol worked at Bank of America, Citibank, Visa International, and Deutsche Bank. Most of her career has been focused on starting new payments products and fostering the adoption of new payments technologies. Carol has also worked with central banks and NGO's on strategies for implementation of new national payments infrastructures.

Email Carol: carol@glenbrook.com
LinkedIn: www.linkedin.com/in/carolcoyebenson

About Glenbrook

Glenbrook Partners is an independent payments industry strategy consulting and research firm. We bring to our clients a unique combination of our specialized skills in payments, many years of hands-on experience in the field, and our global network of professional relationships. Coupled with our payments training capabilities, Glenbrook is an ideal partner for an organization evaluating its next steps in payments. Our projects are cost efficient and high impact.

Glenbrook serves payments professionals in many different kinds of companies, including payments services providers, card networks, technology, risk management companies, banks, merchants, and treasury managers.

In addition to Glenbrook's payments strategy consulting, Glenbrook runs a Payments Education Program which includes its acclaimed Glenbrook Payments Boot Camp®. Through this unique program, Glenbrook shares its experience and insights with payments professionals eager to understand industry fundamentals and direction.

Information about Glenbrook: www.glenbrook.com

Why We Wrote This Book!

The global payments industry huge—and complex. Each country, each payments provider, and each payments user is confronted with multiple choices. The industry is also changing rapidly, as it adopts to new technologies, risk management protocols, and customer preferences. Some of these changes are infrastructural, with central banks in particular driving the global move to real-time payments. Other changes are driven by commercial players, large and small, offering cascading innovations that have come to be known as "fintech".

In Glenbrook's strategy consulting work, we have observed that many of our clients find it challenging to understand the "big picture"—how all the moving parts fit together. Our education program and our books address this need. Our first book, *Payments Systems in the U.S.*, has become the go-to reference book for people seeking to understand how the world's largest, and most complex national payments ecosystem works. *Global Payments* extends this to explain how all country payments systems work, and how, in particular, the confusing, rapidly changing, (and risky!) cross-border payments ecosystem functions.

As we work around the globe, we've been fascinated to observe—and study—how many of the major changes in payments are unfolding in the same way in many countries. But of course, there are leaders (and laggards) among the countries, with some clear stars: the world has a lot to learn from these examples, and *Global Payments* highlights many of these.

Thanks!

The author would like to thank my Glenbrook team members; we continue to learn from each other and support each other in this challenging business. And many thanks are due to our customers, who continue to serve up complex problems and intriguing opportunities for us to contemplate.

Share your feedback!

We welcome your feedback on this book—just send us an email and we'll get back to you! Email: books@glenbrook.com

Table of Contents

Table of Figures

Introduction

PAYMENTS ARE UNIVERSAL. Countries vary in size, wealth, population, and level of technology use, but people and organizations have the same fundamental payments needs. People need to pay other people, pay merchants small and large, and pay bills. People need to get paid—by other people, by employers, by governments. Enterprises need to be paid by their customers, and to pay suppliers and employees. Governments and their agencies need to collect payments from, and disburse payments to, people and organizations. **The essential requirements of payments users are also universal: safety, ubiquity, reliability, affordability, and usability.**

It's not surprising, then, that payments systems around the world have many important similarities. Think of the concept of cash—every country has it, and it works pretty much the same way everywhere.

Of course, there are important differences among countries. Per capita usage of payments systems varies tremendously, and the details of how those systems operate, and are regulated, can differ significantly by country.

This book explores payments system models in countries around the world, including the basic constructs of each system and their significant variations. But payments transcend borders. The flow of cross-border payments is enormous, and **cross-border payments services are among the most complex (and lucrative) sectors of the payments industry**. We explain how cross-border payments work, and how their systems connect to domestic payments systems.

Ten years ago, when Glenbrook published *Payments Systems in the United States*, the focus was on the basics—how the core payments systems (cards, ACH, wires, checks, etc.) work—followed by a relatively short section on payments innovations. That book, now in its third edition, continues to help our clients understand the core systems underlying the world's largest payments ecosystem. And in that third edition, we introduced some key concepts in emerging payments innovation.

> **One measure of the size of the fintech phenomenon:** The Monetary Authority of Singapore—the city-state's central bank—holds an annual fintech conference. In 2019, that event included 60,000 participants from more than 140 countries.

This book is different; it covers the basics, but focuses on innovation, including this decade's "fintech wave." And while some aspects of today's fintech landscape are merely window dressing, others will change our industry substantially.

In this book, we propose a framework for thinking about global payments innovations, and discuss examples of each type. We then pose three big questions we believe the industry will need to study in coming years:

- What will be the balance between country infrastructure and commercial interests?

- What will the future of "open banking" look like for the payments industry?

- How will risk management and fraud control change in an evolving payments ecosystem?

We have an overarching hypothesis about innovation in global payments: It may be that payments systems developments in emerging economies are more important, as predictors of the eventual direction of the global industry, than innovations elsewhere.

This may seem counterintuitive, given the abundance of innovation in more developed economies (Apple Pay! Ethereum!), but the former may very well leapfrog over the latter. Countries without entrenched digital payments systems are using new technologies and business models to define a significantly different world. Many governments with a passionate commitment to financial inclusion see the potential to bring underserved citizens into the digital mainstream—and more economies may come to embrace these models in coming years.

National Payments Systems: An Overview

PAYMENTS SYSTEMS ARE INHERENTLY NATIONAL. Each moves money denominated in a primary national currency, in compliance with laws and regulations set by its home country.

There are no true global payments systems, although as we will see, many products and services create the effect of a nearly global system. And cryptocurrencies could still become true global payments systems; we'll explore that possibility. But as today virtually all payments transactions are national, we'll start there.

What makes a payments system national? It helps to understand that there are **two fundamentally different types of payments: token-based and account-based.**

Token-Based Payments

In token-based payments, value is held in discrete tokens. Cash is the prime example. Cash is issued by a country or, as in Europe and West Africa, by regions choosing to act as such for currency purposes.

Entities allowed to create tokens are closely controlled by national regulations, and often restricted to one or two national institutions given the responsibility to mint coins or print bills. One point of friction is whether this responsibility is controlled primarily by national economic policy or national political concerns.

As a token-based payments system, cash has several unique characteristics. Most importantly, **cash is a self-clearing and self-settling payment method**. Although the use of cash does have costs, such as handling costs and theft risk, it is widely perceived, at least by consumers and small merchants, to be cost-free. In most countries, it is almost universally accepted. It is easy to see how much you have, and equally easy to display that to others. And of course, it is anonymous—a characteristic of enormous importance to some users, and little to none for others.

In 1994, Sanwa Bank in Japan introduced **"money laundering"**—ATMs that sanitize and press bills before dispensing them. According to one report, "the Clean ATMs, as they are known, dispense yen notes that, while not quite as crisp as newly minted ones, are nearly wrinkle-free."

Account-Based Payments

In account-based payments, a party has a bank account, or perhaps a credit card account, prepaid card account, or account with a mobile money provider. The money in such accounts is not a token; rather, it is a promise on the part of the account provider that it owes the account holder that amount of money. These promises are usually backed up in some way—by some form of government insurance, for example, or by a regulatory requirement that the keeper of such funds back them with a trust account at another institution.

All account-based payments are instructions that result in one account being debited and another credited. **Payments systems formalize how this occurs.**

Which entities are allowed to hold accounts, and to participate in payments systems, is closely controlled by national regulation. Only certain types of chartered or licensed financial institutions are allowed to offer accounts, and only those within a country are allowed to join its payments systems.

Key Definition

We use the term *transaction account* to refer to a currency-denominated account offered by a bank or non-bank licensed within a country to hold such accounts. Transaction accounts hold value and can be used to make and receive payment transactions. We include in this definition credit accounts that can be used for the same purposes. The term *financial services providers* (FSPs) refers to providers of these accounts, including banks, e-money issuers, and other licensed institutions.

While each country has its own payments systems (and its own payments systems regulation), **the core payments systems in each country are actually very similar.** One reason for this is the mutual threshold of available technologies and ideas; another is that global standards bodies, such as CPMI (the Committee on Payments and Market Infrastructures) of the Bank for International Settlements (BIS) and the Financial Action Task Force (FATF), create models and standards for how payments systems should work and be regulated. Many entities look to see if a country's payments systems meet these global standards.

Interoperable Payments Systems

Every country has a set of core interoperable payments systems. These systems allow participating financial institutions to issue and accept payments orders that debit one customer's account and credit another's. Most of these systems are open loop, or interoperable.

Interoperable payments systems include electronic and paper-based systems, systems operating in batch and in real time, and systems tailored for low-value and high-value transactions. These all work on the same common architecture: end users, including consumers and enterprises of all types, have account relationships with the financial institutions that hold their transaction accounts. These financial institutions participate—either voluntarily or by government mandate—in the interoperable payments systems, which effect the switching of transactions from one institution to another, and enable settlement of financial obligations among system participants.

ACH systems, direct debit systems, credit transfer systems, faster payments systems, RTGS (real-time gross settlement) systems, and debit card systems are all examples of interoperable systems, as are some credit card, prepaid card, and mobile payments systems.

Interoperable Payments System

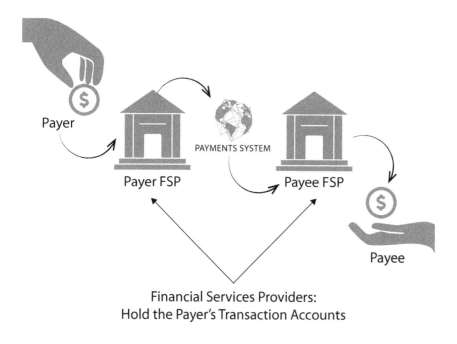

Financial Services Providers:
Hold the Payer's Transaction Accounts

Figure 2-1: Interoperable Payments System

In contrast, in **closed-loop systems**, a payments services provider has a direct business relationship (and provides transaction accounts to) both payer and payee. As with open-loop systems, account holders can be consumers, enterprises, or merchants. Payment transactions here are simply book entries on the provider's part, debiting one party and crediting another. Closed-loop systems include some credit card providers—for example, American Express in its original model—mobile money services such as M-PESA in Kenya, and account-holding wallet providers such as Alipay in China.

When a bank is the provider in question, transactions are considered **on-us**. Note that closed-loop systems almost always rely on either open-loop systems or cash to put money into, or take money out of, the system's transaction accounts.

Differences Across Countries

Although payments systems are similar across countries, there are also major differences. **Consumer and enterprise use of such systems varies widely.** On the consumer side in particular, an important factor is the percentage of adults holding transaction accounts with FSPs; this can range from the low 20s in some developing countries to the high 90s in some developed countries. Payments use by type also varies greatly. Some countries remain stubbornly cash-based while others are populated by enthusiastic users of credit cards; some never use checks, while others often do. Although there are certainly global trends toward use of digital payments, there is significant variation across countries, in not only the rate of change but also the type of digital payments adopted.

The Players

Despite their differences, each country's payments ecosystem includes similar types of players.

- **Financial services providers** (FSPs), including banks, chartered e-money issuers, microfinance institutions, and other chartered specialty financial services companies. Most FSPs provide customers with transaction accounts along with the ability to make payments into, and out of, those accounts.

- A **central bank** typically regulates each country's payments systems, though the extent of its powers varies. The central bank almost always operates its country's RTGS wire transfer system, and often other systems, including a national RTRP (real-time retail payments) system. Central bank representatives often sit on payments clearing house boards, in advisory roles. Many central banks also manage national currencies.

- Many countries have one or more **clearing houses** involved with the operations of national payments systems. These institutions are often owned collectively by all of a country's financial institutions—or perhaps more typically, by its largest institutions. Clearing houses may operate ACH (direct debit and credit transfer) systems, ATM or national debit card systems, and checking systems; some now operate RTRP systems. In recent years, some clearing houses have been privatized.

- All countries have a **card system**. Debit and credit cards may be provided through a domestic card scheme (operated by a multipurpose clearing house or a dedicated entity) and/or by global card networks. ATM cards normally function as debit cards. Global card networks, if present in a given country, may operate their platforms either locally or from outside it, on a regional or even global basis.

- **Processors**, which may be global or local, provide on-behalf-of services to banks, other FSPs, payments system operators, and end users. These payments software providers help banks and other FSPs run internal payments operations and connect (directly or through processors) to payments systems.

- **Payments services providers**, sometimes called aggregators or processors, exist in every country. Their functions and permissions vary widely—as does the terminology used. Often, providers offer specialized merchant services such as bill payments and card acquisition. Many stand under the "fintech umbrella" discussed in Chapter 5.

Confusion Alert

The term *payments services provider* (PSP) has no standard global definition; like general terms such as *aggregator, gateway,* and *wallet,* it's used very differently in different jurisdictions. We recommend focusing on what an individual entity or group is actually doing, not what it's called.

National Payments Systems: A Common Model

THIS SECTION DESCRIBES THE core, or basic, payments systems typical in almost all countries. Newer systems and innovations on the core are discussed later on.

Basic Constructs of Interoperable Systems

Core payments systems are differentiated by characteristics including ownership and governance, functionality, and participant economics.

Major differences include:

- Who owns, governs, and operates the system
- What types of interoperability are supported
- Push or pull payments
- How payments are initiated
- Whether payments are processed in batches or individually in real time
- The economic model the system operates under
- How financial settlement between institutions is handled
- Supported use cases
- Transaction revocability and fraud management

Key Components of an Interoperable Payments System

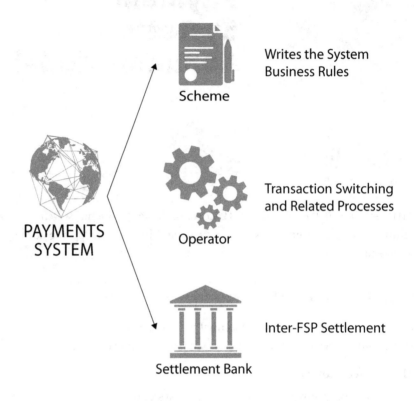

Figure 3-1: Key Components of an Interoperable Payments System

Ownership, Governance, and Operation

- Multiple system components may be owned by a single entity. In Mexico's SPEI system, for example, the central bank provides the scheme, writes the rules, operates the transaction switching platform, and handles inter-FSP settlement. In other countries, a given entity, such as India's NPCI or the UK's PayUK, may control and operate multiple schemes. Often, these entities are owned by groups of banks, with some central bank involvement.

- One entity may own and control the scheme, while another, chosen by the scheme, acts as operator—for example, Peru's BIM system.

- One entity may own and control the scheme, specifying how operator(s) must exchange transactions, but leaving operator choice up to FSPs. The EU's complex SEPA payments systems are an example here.

- Inter-FSP settlement always requires a settlement bank. If a system is not bank-owned and -operated, a scheme will identify a settlement bank and process. Most interoperable payments systems use the country's central bank here, though exceptions exist.

- Many interoperable payments systems are owned cooperatively, by clearing houses, or groups of FSPs (usually banks). Others are provided directly by government or quasi-government entities. Still others, notably most global card networks, are commercial enterprises. At Glenbrook, we distinguish between "thick" and "thin" payments systems, depending on how much functionality they offer FSPs; this tends to correlate with cooperative/public vs. private ownership. Thick systems often have highly detailed rulebooks.

Interoperability Support

Interoperability describes how participating FSPs exchange transactions, through scheme-defined services, with each other. It's usually achieved in one of three ways:

- **Scheme interoperability** is the most common method, and what most people think of when they hear the term. Participating FSPs are bound by a common set of business rules defining how transactions are exchanged. There are two types of scheme interoperability, one using a single switch and the other multiple switches governed under a single set of rules. RTGS systems, most ACH systems, and most open-loop card systems use the single switch model; the US's ACH system and Europe's SEPA systems use the multiple-switch model.

- **Network interoperability** exists when two payments schemes negotiate an exchange agreement. Each has its own rules, and its own switch or operating platforms; a "meta-agreement" defines how physical interoperation occurs and specifies transaction rules for given circumstances. Many ATM networks use network interoperability to connect regional ATM switches. It's also used for cross-border and cross-regional card payments—allowing the holder of a domestic credit card, for example, to use that card in another country. It's seldom used by network members competing in a single market, however, as it opens a market to out-of-network banks.

- **Parallel system interoperability** creates the effect of interoperability for end customers of two schemes, without actual interoperation. In the US, this allows merchants accepting consumer card payments to participate in more than one scheme, with a commercial service provider acting as intermediary. While the card networks don't actually interoperate, the merchant experience is largely consistent, made possible by products and systems provided by card acquirers and processors.

Push or Pull Payments

Push or pull payments is a confusing but important distinction. A push payment is entered into the payments system by the payer's FSP, and requires knowledge of the payee's account credentials, as with wire transfers, credit transfer systems, and RTRP systems. Push payments don't bounce, as the sending FSP already knows whether the customer has money.

In contrast, a pull payment is entered into the payments system by the payee's FSP, and requires knowledge of the payer's account credentials. Card payments, checks, and ACH direct debits are pull payments. They can bounce (unless, as with card systems, there is an added authorization transaction).

Confusion Alert

The issue of push vs. pull payments is not a question of customer authorization, which all payments systems require before an account is debited; both push and pull systems may also allow standing authorizations. In modern RTRP systems, a protocol known as *request to pay* or *request for payment* is emerging. While sometimes described as a pull payment, this it is, in fact, a "request to push."

Payment Initiation

This can seem like a defining feature: card payments are made by cards, checks by paper, and so forth. But each system supports specific initiation types and channels, which can change over time. For example, some card payments are now made by mobile phone, and some check payments by digital image.

An important function of payments system rules is to specify initiation types, at times in considerable detail. Card systems using chips, for example, have detailed specifications as to what the chip actually does. A system supporting preauthorized transactions, such as a direct debit system used for bill payment, will have rules specifying which FSP (the payer's or the payee's) is financially responsible for securing payer authorization. Some payments systems support multiple initiation methods, but apply different rules depending on method; the distinction between "card present" and "card not present" in card system rules is an example.

It's All About the Rules

Scheme rules—sometimes referred to as *business rules* or *operating rules*—are very important in payments systems. Rules define the obligations and responsibilities of FSPs in interoperable payments systems, and of payers and payees in closed-loop systems.

Rules of an interoperable system define, among other topics:

- Which types of FSPs may join the system, and requirements for joining
- Processes for ongoing governance and rules management
- How the platform operates, using which message standards
- Obligations of FSPs and the platform
- Supported use cases, along with required or optional processes for each
- Liabilities of all parties, to the system and to each other
- Exception, fraud, and dispute management
- What scheme and interchange fees apply, and how they're collected
- How the system supports third-party access and/or connects to other systems

It should be noted that private scheme operating or business rules often overlap with national law and regulation. Schemes whose platforms are operated by third parties also have platform operating guidelines. Any of these documents may control aspects of system operations and the obligations of involved parties.

Rules and Regulation

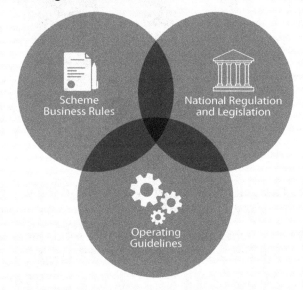

Batch vs. Real-Time Processing

For many years, virtually all retail payments systems operated in batch mode, meaning that payments transactions moved between financial institutions and payments systems in groups, rather than individually. Checks and ACH (direct debits and credit transfers) were batch processed. Cards were (and still are) a hybrid—real-time authorization followed by batch clearing. Only wholesale wire transfer systems operated entirely in real time.

Today, most countries have either implemented or are implementing real-time push retail payments systems (often referred to as "faster payments systems") designed to deposit funds into the payee's transaction account in near-real time.

Economic Model

As you can imagine, this is a complicated topic. It may help to consider it in terms of the fee types in any given interoperable payments system.

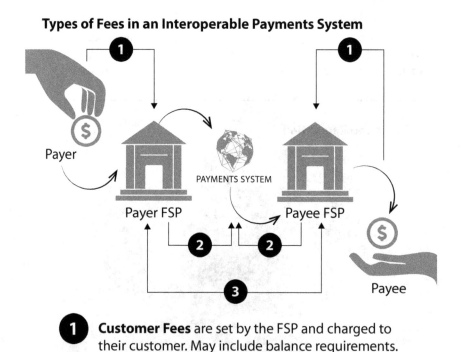

Types of Fees in an Interoperable Payments System

1 **Customer Fees** are set by the FSP and charged to their customer. May include balance requirements.

2 **Processing and Scheme Fees** are set by the Payments System and charged to the FSPs.

3 **Interchange Fees** are set by the Payments System and are paid by one FSP to the other FSP.

Figure 3-2: Type of Fees in an Interoperable Payments System

Customer fees. In general, interoperable payments system rules don't specify or control customer fees, which are defined by each end customer's FSP. Customer fees, of course, may be affected by the fees FSPs pay to either the payments system or another FSP. In a number of countries, the government has stepped in to set limits on end-user fees, or abolish them altogether, typically to further financial inclusion.

Customer fees may be flat, or a percentage of value. They may be expressed as balance requirements rather than fees. FSPs, particularly banks, often provide a certain number of free payments transactions as part of a product bundle such as a transaction account. Any FSP handling a high volume of payments made or received by a customer, however, is likely to charge fees for that service.

Processing fees. Any entity operating a transaction switch charges some kind of transaction processing fee. Around the world, the value range of these fees is huge, running from fractions of a US cent to many times that amount. Unsurprisingly, it's a question of volume. About 1 billion transactions per year are necessary to drive processing fees below one cent per transaction—a threshold of great importance in emerging economies trying to reduce the use of cash.

Interchange fees. These are the source of much controversy and confusion in the payments industry. In an interoperable transaction, an interchange fee is paid by one FSP to the other. Some payments systems charge interchange and others don't; those that do generally define it in scheme rules. Systems with no interchange are said to clear "at par."

The amount and direction of an interchange fee (that is, which FSP pays which) can vary; this too is set by scheme rules. Wires, checks, and most ACH direct debit and credit transfer systems don't use interchange, while card systems generally do. The jury is still out on new mobile and faster payments systems—some use it, some don't. The practice of interchange has drawn the attention of competition authorities worldwide and, in situations where regulators feel it is being abused, limits have been put on such fees.

In card systems, used primarily for consumer-to-merchant payments, interchange flows from the merchant's FSP to the consumer's FSP. The merchant's FSP then charges the merchant a customer fee to cover the required interchange fee. In markets such as Mexico and Thailand, where new faster payments systems are being used for merchant payments, governments have barred FSPs from charging merchants fees on low-value transactions. In such cases, there is no interchange. Where interchange rates are relatively high, it's common for the FSP incurring such a charge to pass it on to the customer. Where rates are lower, these costs are often absorbed by the FSP.

Non-fee revenue and adjacencies. In many countries, customers are charged no explicit transaction fees, as payers or payees. The FSP in these cases is recouping costs, and possibly making a profit, from related service fees or revenue sources such as account balances. The most typical, and most lucrative, of these "adjacencies" is lending: account balances (arguably there because of incoming and outgoing payments) are used by the bank to lend money, profitably, to other customers.

Challenge

As faster payments systems come into use by merchants worldwide, other fee issues will need to be resolved. Especially in emerging economies, many people believe that electronic payments cannot succeed if small and poor merchants must pay fees, and that FSPs will need to support their business models with adjacencies such as lending or data monetization. While this can work, it doesn't address the possibility of commerce fraud on the part of merchants. Card systems make a merchant's FSP financially responsible for such fraud, with financial liability covered by merchant fees. How will this be resolved in the new systems?

Inter-Institution Financial Settlement

This once behind-the-scenes aspect of interoperable payments is seeing a surge of innovation. Inter-institution settlements are those between institutions (rather than between an FSP and its customers), and are defined by scheme rules. Most retail interoperable payments systems use "net settlement," in which the scheme system operator calculates the net position of each FSP as sender or receiver of funds throughout the settlement window (normally a business day). When the window closes, each FSP's net position is posted to its account at a designated settlement bank.

Confusion Alert

The term *retail*, when used in payments systems, refers not to retail store transactions, but to relatively low-value transactions, in which a consumer is typically payer or payee. *Wholesale*, in contrast, typically refers to high-value transactions between institutions. A given payments system is considered retail or wholesale, though there is no clearly defined cutoff point between the two designations.

Most wholesale payments systems (such as wire transfer systems) are real-time gross settlement (RTGS) systems, in which each individual transaction is posted to the FSP's bank account at the designated settlement account as it occurs.

Supported Use Cases

Many payments systems start out with a target use case. The original card payments systems, for example, targeted restaurant purchases, and many mobile payments systems target person-to-person (P2P) payments. But use cases inevitably expand, driven both by consumer demand—as consumers get used to using a new system for one purpose and want to use it for others—and by the economics of payments processing, which favors high volumes at the switch.

Virtually all mature payments systems, both interoperable and closed loop, have come to support all or most of what we at Glenbrook call the "domains of payment."

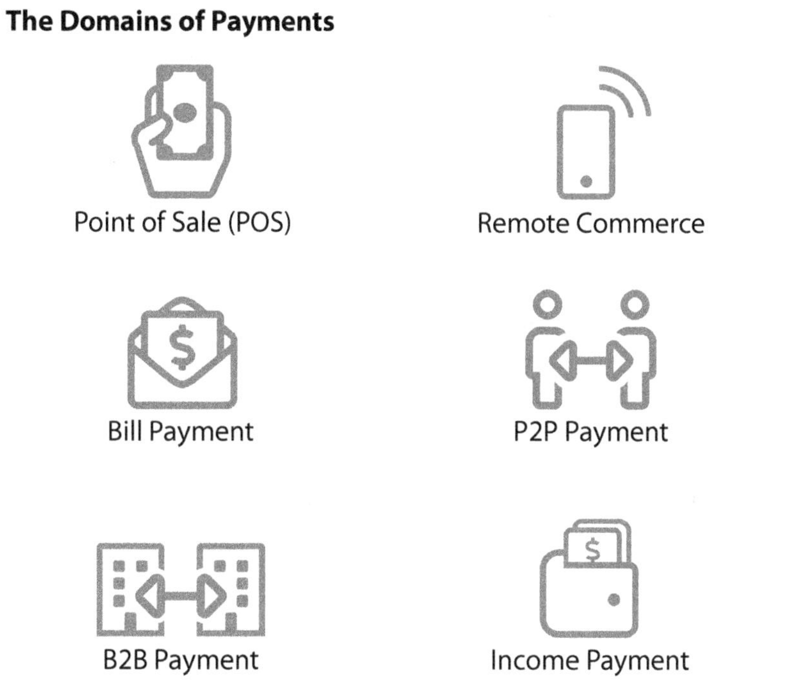

The Domains of Payments

Point of Sale (POS)

Remote Commerce

Bill Payment

P2P Payment

B2B Payment

Income Payment

Figure 3-3: The Domains of Payments

Transaction Revocability and Fraud Management

This is another complex area, with significant differences among payments systems. At the most abstract, the question is to what extent a payments system—through its scheme rules—defines how FSPs handle transaction liability, exception processing, and fraud management. Most checking and ACH systems, for example, set minimal parameters, leaving most decisions—and work— to the FSPs. Others, notably the card payments systems, set detailed rules and procedures.

Transaction revocability is often discussed as an attribute of a transaction itself. But it is actually a scheme rule defining whether or not a payer has a right to claim that a transaction was unauthorized. Several transaction and authorization parameters may support, or not support, such a rule. For example, a biometrically authorized payment transaction may be used in a system whose rule says payers may not reverse such transactions.

Payments systems vary widely in prescriptiveness here. Most open-loop card networks have detailed regulations specifying how banks using the system handle customer disputes and complaints, requirements for end-user transaction authentication, and a wide range of other security issues. At the other end of the spectrum, most checking and ACH systems leave the majority of these responsibilities up to FSPs.

Of particular note is how payments systems handle commerce fraud. While payment fraud is unauthorized access to a payer's transaction account in order to conduct a transaction, commerce fraud is when a merchant fails to provide promised goods, or supplies defective or fraudulent goods or services. In most countries, card network rules make the merchant's bank responsible for much commerce fraud; this works well but creates a financial burden on the merchant's bank that translates to high merchant fees. An open question is how commerce fraud will be managed in faster payments systems, particularly those in emerging economies where poor merchants may resist electronic payments charges.

Core Payments Systems Across Countries

Core payments systems in most countries have similar functionality, though delivery particulars and per capita usage vary.

Checks

Checking, while considered an out-of-date payments system, has played an important role in the economic development of many modern nations. It was **the original interoperable payments system**: the receiver of a check could deposit it into her bank, though it was written on another bank. An elaborate and expensive system of clearing checks (returning them to the bank of the checkwriter) has evolved over time, with some parts being automated and others, such as delivery of paper checks, remaining stubbornly manual. In recent years, variations on check imaging technology have made bank-to-bank clearing infrastructure largely electronic, turning checks into paper orders for an electronic process. Despite these improvements, the global trend is away from checks and toward fully electronic processes.

There are several aspects of checking to keep in mind as payments systems become fully electronic. One is **the role of bank-owned clearing associations**, many of which have taken on a processing role in interoperable digital payments systems including ACH systems, debit card and ATM networks, and faster payments systems. The other factor to remember about checking is its **ease of use**. An individual or businesses checkwriter doesn't need to know anything about the payee, other than name (and to be technical, not even that); a note in the memo field tracks what each payment is for. Checks also clear at par, with no interchange charged between the paying and depository institutions.

ACH

ACH (automated clearing house) systems evolved out of checking systems and check clearing houses in most large cities. Today, ACH systems are both fully electronic and batch oriented. They preserve some of the advantages of the checking system (notably, by connecting all banks in a country). Unlike checking, however, **communication is electronic and processing and clearing systems simple and uniform**. Where all checks are pull payments, ACH systems support both pull payments (here called *direct debits*), and push payments (called *credit transfers*).

ACH began as, and is still dominated by, high-volume, recurring payments and pre-established transaction flows. Direct deposit of payroll, pension, and benefit payments (credit transfers) and regular monthly bill payments (direct debits) still account for the bulk of ACH transactions in most systems. Payment of business supplier bills (credit transfers) are also high-volume applications.

In recent years, ACH systems have also been enabled for one-time or ad hoc payments, particularly for online bill payment and remote commerce. Though these payments are ordered in online or real-time environments, they clear and settle in batch. In countries such as the US, this process has been speeded up ("same-day ACH"), but is still not real-time.

ACH systems are inexpensive workhorses. Many ACH operators charge participating banks fractions of a US cent for handling each payment. Most have no or very low interchange rates, on only certain payment types. ACH direct debit payments, however, have additional costs for end customers: Like checks, they can bounce for insufficient funds, and they may be reversed if unauthorized by the paying customer. ACH credit transfer payments do not have these risks.

Real-Time Retail Payments (RTRP, aka Faster Payments)

RTRP systems deliver immediate payments, based on electronic messaging from phones or other devices. Most RTRP systems are interoperable among a set of FSPs, but others are closed loop. RTRP systems are designed to work continuously, providing messaging to sending and receiving parties 24/7. Many, originally designed to support P2P payments, have expanded to address use cases including bill payment, business-to-business (B2B) payments, salary and benefits payments, and purchases. Rapidly becoming "core" in many markets, RTRP systems are discussed in detail in Chapter 6.

Debit Cards

In much of the developed world, debit cards are the primary in-store payment method. The debit card processing model evolved from two roots: open-loop credit cards and interconnected ATM networks. Today, almost all retail banks, in all countries, participate in one or more debit card schemes, which provide interoperability among bank accounts and are most often used for consumer payments to merchants and billers.

Debit cards are pull payments. They use real-time authorization messaging followed by batch clearing and settlement. Like credit cards, they use interchange fees to compensate the consumer's bank from the merchant's bank, which passes that charge on to the merchant; in many countries, regulators have restricted these merchant charges. Debit cards generally offer consumers some protection from commerce fraud. Banks typically offer debit cards as a part of transaction account "bundles," with no specific charge for their use.

As debit cards have become prevalent, many countries have put their use under national control. Though international card brands were (and remain) eager to provide their debit card products in these countries, banks and regulators have developed national debit card schemes; these generally have become a country's preferred, if not only, debit networks. Canada's Interac and India's RuPay are examples.

Prepaid Cards

Interoperable prepaid cards carry a card network brand and can be used just like debit cards wherever that network brand is accepted. Rather than debiting a bank account, however, a prepaid card debits an account balance maintained by the prepaid card processor, working on behalf of the card's sponsor.

The sponsor, generally a brand familiar to consumers, keeps the balance of funds received from the consumer in a commercial bank, which often acts as issuer from the card network's perspective.

Closed-loop prepaid cards are not interoperable. They are generally the liability of one issuer (often a merchant) and usable only at that merchant's outlets.

Kudos: The global card industry, from its infancy, has done a stellar job of ensuring global interoperability through both rules and technology. Standardized mag stripes (now seen as outdated technology) were a triumph of standardization in their day. Today, the extension of card network global protocols into chip cards, NFC, QR codes, and other realms continues this admirable practice.

Credit Cards

Credit cards, the first product of the global card networks, remain popular with consumers in affluent countries. Their overall transaction volume, particularly when measured by "count" rather than "amount," has diminished as their debit card offspring have grown.

Credit cards, like debit cards, are pull instruments, characterized by real-time authorization and batch clearing and settlement. The economics of credit cards are dominated by interest on revolving loans (they've been called the most profitable product in the history of banking) and, for interoperable card networks, by interchange the merchant's bank pays to the issuing bank. Issuers compete on lending rates and, in particular, on the types and richness of their consumer reward programs.

In addition to interoperable credit card networks such as Visa, Mastercard, and UnionPay, there are closed-loop card networks such as American Express; today, many of these have hybrid arrangements making them semi-open-loop. The acquiring side of the card industry is highly developed, making it easy for merchants to accept a wide range of card types. Finally, private-label credit cards, each used at only one merchant, are often processed by the same institutions that serve open-loop issuers and acquirers.

Today, credit cards, like debit cards, may be used at the point of sale or remotely—via a physical card, smartphone-based digital wallet, or another device such as a smart watch or ring.

Wires and RTGS

Longstanding wire transfer systems use a design approach very close to that of new RTRP systems. Usually offered by a country's central bank, these real-time, electronic, and interoperable messaging systems debit one account held by a bank at the central bank and credit another. Like any book-transfer transaction, these need no after-the-fact settlement—a transaction settles as it is posted to each bank's account at the central bank. This process is called *gross settlement*, and these systems collectively are called RTGS (real-time gross settlement) systems.

Unlike RTRP systems, wire systems are designed to operate at high transaction values. In the US alone, they account for over $1 quadrillion a year, with an average transaction size of more than $4 million. While high-volume retail payments systems expect a certain amount of error and fraud, it is easy to see that a wire transfer system's ability to accept fraud on a $500 million transfer is essentially zero. This makes these transactions expensive; while the processing model is simple, costly "wraps" of software, people, and processes are essential safeguards.

Wire systems often run on older technology, and in many countries are available only during "banking hours."

Typical Characteristics of National Interoperable Payments Systems

	Checks	Credit Cards	Dedit Cards	ACH	Wire Transfer (RTGS)	Real-Time Retail Payments
Ownership/Control	Banks	Commercial Entity	Commercial or Cooperative	Cooperative Government	Central Bank or Cooperative	Varies!
Push or Pull	Pull	Pull	Pull	Pull (direct debit) Push (credit transfer)	Push	Push
Initiation	Paper	Card, electronic	Card, mobile, other	Batch file submissions	Electronic	Electronic
Clearing	Image or Paper	Electronic	Electronic	Electronic	Electronic	Electronic
Pre-authorized Option?	No	Yes	Yes	Yes	No	Yes
Processing Type	Batch	Hybrid Real-Time/Batch	Hybrid Real-Time/Batch	Batch	Real-Time	Real-Time
Economic Model	Clear at Par	Interchange	Interchange	Par or Interchange	Par	Par or Interchange
Settlement	Net	Net	Net	Net	Gross	Varies!
Fraud Management	Up to FSPs	FSPs and System	FSPs and System	Up to FSPs	Up to FSPs	TBD

A more detailed description of these payments system types is given in Glenbrook's book, *Payments Systems in the U.S.*

Table 3-1: Typical Characteristics of National Interoperable Payments Systems

Cross-Border Payments

CROSS-BORDER PAYMENTS IS A complex topic, and one prone to misunderstanding. Perhaps not coincidentally, it is also the most lucrative area of the payments industry, characterized by a perpetual battle between incumbents and startups.

Customer needs for cross-border payments span all six domains of payments:

- Point of Sale (POS)—purchases by travelers or expatriates paying from accounts in their home countries

- Remote Commerce—people and business making online purchases from merchants in another country

- Bill Payment—people paying bills for family members in other countries

- P2P Payment—notably migrant workers sending money home to family and friends

- B2B Payment—businesses paying businesses for goods or services bought in another country

- Income Payment—businesses and governments paying salaries or benefits to individuals in another country

Although all of these domains are important, the largest by far is the B2B payment flow, which grows as globalization drives more and more businesses to sell—and to source purchases—from other countries.

Why Cross-Border Payments Are Misunderstood

Domestic, account-based payments systems work when a payment order results in the debiting of one transaction account and the crediting of another. These domestic systems transfer money between banks, or other licensed transaction account providers; the accounts involved are denominated in that country's currency. The ability to provide such accounts is governed by national regulation, with only FSPs licensed in that country, by that country's regulators, allowed to provide transaction accounts and to participate in domestic payments systems.

One might imagine that cross-border payments work much like domestic payments, with some global payments system debiting one transaction account in one country and crediting another in another country. But no such system exists.

The often hard-to-understand truth is that money never leaves its country—except, as we say, in a suitcase. It may appear to do so: you make a cross-border payment and have less money in your account, and the happy recipient in the other country has more money in theirs. But the reality is more complex.

How Cross-Border Payments Work

All cross-border payments rely on some entity (usually but not always a bank) that is content to have its account in one country increase in value, while another entity in another country (again, usually a bank), with which it has a business relationship of some sort, is content to see an account it owns in its country reduced in value.

> **SWIFT** is the dominant provider of financial institution messaging services for cross-border payments. Its standardized messages allow bank correspondents to "speak the same language." SWIFT itself is not a payments system and not a party to any exchange of value.

Typically, this is done through **correspondent banking**. Two banks enter into a private agreement to become international correspondents. Each opens an account at the other bank (known as *nostro* and *vostro* accounts), and each transfers money into that account from another domestic account in the same country. The banks agree to account terms including balance requirements, overdraft permissions, and transaction handling fees. Typically, they use SWIFT, a global financial services messaging service, to communicate about transactions executed under this agreement.

A Cross-Border Example

Say Alpha, a company in Argentina, wants to pay its supplier Beta in Belgium:

- Alpha has an account with Argentina Commercial Bank (ACB). Alpha notifies ACB that it wants to transfer money to Beta, and provides the account number of Beta at Belgium Commercial Bank (BCB).

- In this example, ACB has a correspondent relationship with BCB. ACB debits Alpha's account, and credits BCB's account, in a book transfer on ACB's books.

- ACB sends a SWIFT message instructing BCB to debit ACB's account on its books and credit Beta's account; this, again, is a book transfer on BCB's books.

- End of transaction! Each bank has reallocated money in its bank from one customer's account to another.

Correspondent Banking

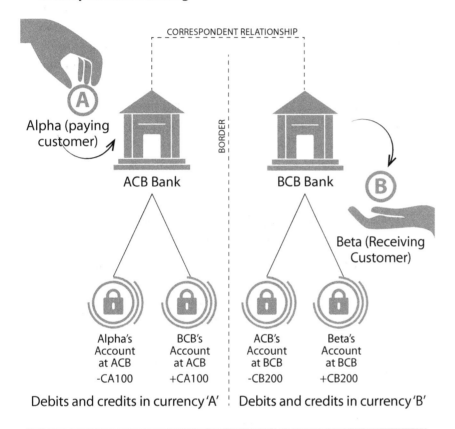

Figure 4-1: Corresponding Banking Model

Common Questions

- **What does BCB do with the money piling up in its account at ACB?** That's up to BCB. It may have enough transactions going in the opposite direction to balance things out. If not, it needs to do something with the money—perhaps loan it to someone who needs currency A, buy something, or sell currency A on the foreign exchange market in exchange for a currency it needs somewhere else.

- **Doesn't ACB run the risk of running out of money in its account at BCB?** Yes, that's a problem. BCB may be willing to extend an overdraft to ACB, but there will be a limit defined in the correspondent banking agreement. ACB's need to keep money in its account at BCB is called the *liquidity cost* of correspondent banking.

- **What if ACB's correspondent (BCB) doesn't have an account with the receiving customer?** That is more common than the super-simple example above. If the end parties have relationships with banks that lack correspondent banking relationships with each other, one bank will use a domestic payments system to send money to a partner—a domestic correspondent bank—that does have a correspondent relationship with the other country. There can be multiple banks in the "chain" on either side of the transaction.

- **Wait a minute—there are two currencies here. Who is doing the currency exchange?** In the example above, one of the two banks does the currency conversion; which one is spelled out in their private business agreement. With multiple banks or providers on either side, one of the entities will have that opportunity. Which one may not be obvious to either the sending or receiving party, or even to their immediate banks. You could also say the "lucky party" gets to do it—currency conversion is normally quite profitable.

- **What kind of fees are involved?** Lots! Every bank or provider in the chain is compensated in some way. The two banks providing transaction accounts to the end customers will likely charge them fees called *exchange markups*. Banks in the middle, which have no direct relationship with the end customers, may simply take a piece of the transaction as it goes through the chain—a practice called *bene deduct* (beneficiary deduct).

- **How do the two customers know when money is debited and credited, and in what amounts?** Historically, customers have not had the ability to influence this—unless they are large corporate clients with a lot of sway over their large corporate banks. This is changing, however; see "The Incumbent Fights Back," later in this chapter.

- **Who makes the rules for correspondent banking?** No one! Each bank is regulated within its own country, and SWIFT messaging has its own rules, but each bank is free to make whatever correspondent banking relationship deals it wants to.

- **This doesn't apply to international money transmitters, does it?** Yes, it does—there are no exceptions. A money transmitter will have a bank account in the sending country and one in the receiving country.

A transmitter using a national payments system to receive money from the payer relies on its bank in that country being connected to a domestic payments system that can receive the payment into its account; the same is true on the disbursement side in the receiving country. Even when transmitters are receiving cash on the sending side and disbursing it on the receiving side, they do so from domestic bank accounts in each country. The difference for international money transmitters is that the bank where the correspondent payments take place is typically not where the funds need to be. The "last mile" of the transaction may be cash pickup at a pharmacy chain, bank agent, or small shop.

> **Very large money transmitters** act as their own correspondents. Rather than relying on a bank that has nostro/vostro relationships with an international correspondent, they have accounts at banks in each country, and oversee those accounts—just like the nostro/vostro accounts of the correspondent banks. If balances get too high or low on either side, they use conventional correspondent banking wire transfers to move money in or out.

- **What about the global card networks? They let me pay in foreign currencies.** The global card networks are very successful in disguising the complexity of these processes from both end customers (payer and merchant) and banks (issuers and acquirers). But the card networks themselves have bank accounts in every country, and maintain balances in those accounts to support net flows of currency into and out of the accounts of their bank customers (for open-loop card networks) or end customers (for closed-loop card networks).

- **What about global banks with branches in many countries?** This is no exception. To participate in domestic payments schemes, a large global bank can't simply have a branch in another country; rather, it needs to have a subsidiary licensed as a bank in that country. To handle cross-border payments, that subsidiary needs *nostro/vostro* accounts with banks in other countries; most global banks make it a policy that those correspondent relationships are with their own subsidiaries in the other country. This helps standardize (and reduce) fee requirements, but doesn't change the basic account debit and credit mechanics necessary to execute transactions.

- **This system seems ripe for fraud—it could be used to launder money or do other nefarious things.** Yes! And regulators are acutely aware of this. Regulators in each country place requirements on banks sending and receiving cross-border payments, and closely supervise their activities.

> **Money Laundering:** Despite efforts by banks in all countries to detect, control, and stop money laundering and related activities, it is generally believed within the industry that most money laundering is not detected.

The Incumbent Fights Back

The correspondent banking model of cross-border payments has long been under attack for being too costly, too slow, and too opaque to meet the needs of most customers. Banks other than the large global players have often found the risks and costs—particularly the liquidity costs—of cross-border payments prohibitively high. This has enabled a wide range of "over-the-top" providers (including money transmitters, global card networks, and wallet providers such as PayPal) to sell solutions to customers while performing correspondent banking transactions "behind the curtain."

More recently, companies such as Ripple have made direct attacks on the correspondent banking model. Central banks including the US Federal Reserve Banks and the Banco de México have also attempted to improve cross-border payments with programs such as Directo a México.

All this has put SWIFT, the infrastructure provider enabling much of the previous model, under serious threat. It's responded by vastly enhancing its model with SWIFT gpi (Global Payment Initiative), improving the speed, transparency, and cost of correspondent banking-based, cross-border payments.

Payments Innovations: An Introduction

IT'S HARD TO MISS **the global fintech revolution.** From massive venture investments to daily headlines, a lot is happening under this umbrella. But what is "fintech"? Glenbrook has spent most of its 20-year existence in this field, which continues to fascinate—and at times bewilder—us as more and more products and services are introduced.

Glenbrook's clients, in our strategy and education practices, are often commercial enterprises trying to make money in the payments industry, or reduce their payments costs while improving efficiency. Increasingly, we also work with governments, NGOs, and national clearing houses seeking to improve their payments infrastructures—often to promote financial inclusion or achieve national goals of enabling a digital ecosystem.

Let's explore what the stakeholders want from payments innovation.

Stakeholder Perspectives

We group stakeholders into three functional categories: users (consumers, merchants, billers, enterprises, and government agencies), providers (banks, networks, processors, service providers, etc.), and other influencers such as regulators and advocacy groups.

Payments Users

- **Consumer payments behavior is driven, we believe, by a combination of utility, safety, convenience, and financial reward**. The utility comes from ubiquity—the ability to pay and be paid by anyone. Ubiquity is often assumed in the developed world, where interoperable payments systems are common. In emerging economies, many of which are today home to rapid fintech innovation, its lack is a significant barrier. Similarly, safety is so assumed in many developed economies that it doesn't show up as a need—but without a strong belief in the safety of funds, no consumer will use an electronic payment product. In fact, we often counsel our clients to be careful about overemphasizing the need for security: once consumers believe their funds are secure, relative security does not appear to drive consumer behavior. Instead, convenience—a combination of speed, ease of use, and financial reward (including lower fees, access to credit, avoidance of penalties, or rewards of some kind) is paramount. We also caution with respect to convenience; while it's critically important, consumers don't change their behavior for minor increases in convenience. Interestingly, in many markets privacy may emerge as a key driver of consumer payments behavior.

> **Very large merchants,** in particular those selling remotely, have increasingly complex payments processing requirements, which often vary significantly by country. Not surprisingly, an industry has emerged to cater to these needs—"global payments services providers" such as Adyen that enable merchants to accept a variety of payments methods, in some cases also managing risk and integration.

- **Merchant payments preferences are complex.** We use the term *merchant* here to include a wide spectrum of payments acceptors of all sizes, including stores (physical and remote), billers, other enterprises, and government agencies. In general, merchants just want to get paid, and will accept almost any form of tender that serves that goal. After that, merchant payment preferences are driven by wanting to sell more while lowering the cost of payments acceptance. Where those two goals are at odds, the benefits of selling more generally take precedence.

- **As payments users, government agencies are much like any other enterprise,** motivated to improve efficiencies and costs, and to reach their constituents as effectively as possible. High volumes make them important stakeholders in many emerging economies.

Payments Providers

- The number and kind of payments providers is growing. Direct providers (which supply products and services to end users, including consumers, merchants, and other enterprises) tend to see payments as a source of direct revenue (transaction fees and related account balances), an enabler of other revenue (sometimes referred to as "adjacencies"), or sometimes both. The most notable of these, in both traditional retail banking and among fintechs, is revenue accrued from lending. Indirect providers include networks, processors, and service providers, which see transaction volume (and volume-driven revenue) as their most important objective.

Other Influencers

- **Governments as regulators** have an increasingly complex job. Their primary motivation is protecting consumers; this includes both protecting consumers' funds and protecting the customers themselves from payments fraud, predatory lending, and unfair pricing. In most countries, the key industry regulators are in the central bank or bank supervisory agency; their task becomes more challenging as innovation drives the number and type of payments services.

  Equally important is protecting the state from the consequences of money laundering and terrorist financing. Government competition authorities are often important in defining the payments landscape. Ministries of finance may be industry regulators, important to the payments industry if, for example, they demand digital receipts to ensure tax collection. Governments also play an important role as champions of financial inclusion; this is discussed in Chapter 10.

- **Consumer advocacy groups** play an important role in payments, particularly with growing concern over fee transparency, data privacy, and localization.

It seems strange to consider criminals as "stakeholders." But payments fraud is a defining part of the industry, and criminals are quick to study payments innovation and capitalize on weak points. While new payments types can quickly be exploited on an individual case basis, the real concern is when criminals figure out how to attack payments systems at scale.

Payments Fintech Framework

What's the best way to think about payments innovation by fintechs? Here we introduce a framework designed to help you understand the phenomenon of payments fintech, and, we hope, separate the signal from the noise.

We find it useful to think of payments systems primarily as **infrastructure** connecting many different parties. Many fintechs are workarounds compensating for inadequate infrastructure; PayPal, for example, may never have gotten its start in the US market in the late 1990s had people been able to pay for auction goods through the existing card networks. Today, many P2P closed-loop wallet products and services compensate for the failure of retail payments systems to easily connect underlying bank accounts; in some countries, they also compensate for the banking infrastructure's inability to reach the whole population.

What happens to these products and services as the underlying infrastructure improves? Which will disappear, and which evolve and survive?

Two additional perspectives—regulatory and technical innovation—help us better understand payments innovation.

- **Regulatory innovation** is often necessary for product and service innovation. It can take many forms: new laws and regulations (for example, permitting additional transaction account or service provider types); regulatory "sandboxes" allowing both incumbents and challengers to experiment with products and technologies without explicit prior changes in regulation); and regulatory forbearance policies that let providers introduce new products before regulation is formalized (demonstrated in many African markets with e-money issuance).

Several regulatory entities have taken market-leading approaches to embrace payments innovation. In 2015, for example, the **Monetary Authority of Singapore** created a Smart Financial Centre where "innovation is pervasive and technology is used widely to increase efficiency, better manage risks, create new opportunities, and improve people's lives."

In 2018, the **Bank of England** launched a fintech hub, citing "clear prospects for new financial technologies to make the financial system more efficient, effective, and resilient." The **Central Bank of Brazil** developed a fintech strategy "to increase competition and foster innovation in the country's banking system."

More recently, the **Bank for International Settlements (BIS),** through the Financial Stability Board (FSB) and **Committee on Payments and Market Infrastructures (CPMI)**, is developing a roadmap to enhance cross-border payments.

- **Technical innovation** is an obvious driver of payment innovation. It can happen at the broad ecosystem level, as with the proliferation of mobile access and cloud hosting. Security technologies (tokenization, for example) and access technologies (NFC and QR codes) are fundamental to fintech. More focused innovations have also catalyzed change, though many do not endure as other technologies outstrip them; examples here are Square's use of the audio jack to "hear" the mag stripe and (this author's favorite) the capability developed by Loop (since acquired by Samsung) that essentially allowed a mobile phone app to convince a terminal that a card mag stripe had been read.

Our framework provides a way to understand fintechs and fintech developments, and to categorize payments innovations. The next sections explore innovations in payments rails, new transaction account providers, new products and services, and so-called over-the-top and out-of the-box solutions.

Payments System Innovation
A Framework for Understanding Fintech

New and Enhanced Payment Rails

New Transaction Account Providers

Product and Service Innovation

'Over the Top' and 'Out of the Box' Solutions

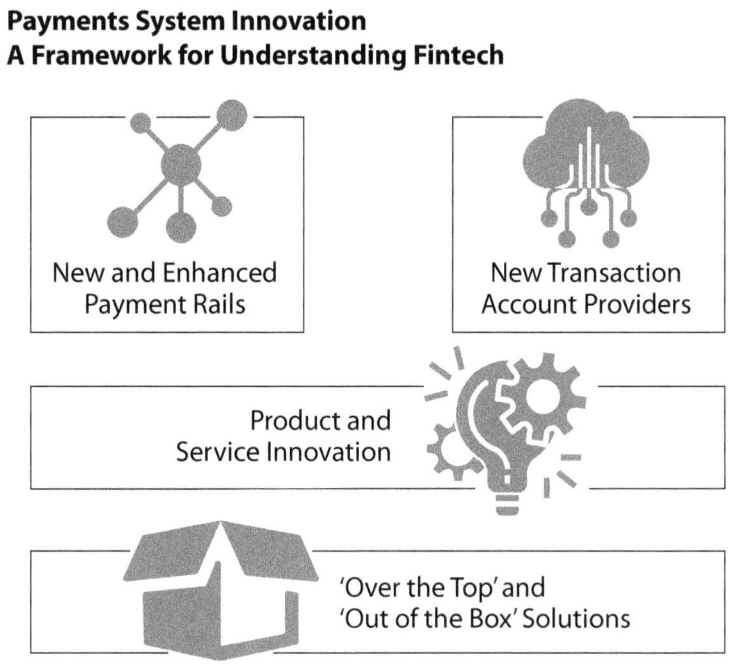

Figure 5-1: Framework for Understanding Fintech Payments System Innovation

Caveat: Any categorization system is by definition imperfect. Many of the examples cited below could be put into several of the categories we define; many companies, products, and services make use of multiple kinds of innovation.

Payments Innovations: The Rails

THE **RAILS** ARE THE core of a payments system. These are primarily interoperable, open-loop systems, although some closed-loop systems may be considered part of a larger overall system. Closed-loop card systems such as American Express, for example, are, along with open-loop systems such as Visa, part of the larger construct "card systems."

The term *rails* is used here to describe an entire system—a scheme and its rules, along with the operating platform on which that system is run. Cards, ACH, checking, and wire systems can all be considered rails. Innovation in rails is seen both with new rails and with enhancements to existing rails. Intriguingly, "regional rails" are now springing up.

Today, most of the focus in the industry is on "faster payments," or new real-time retail payments (RTRP) rails put in place around the world—for example, Faster Payments in the UK, UPI in India, FAST in Singapore, and RTP in the US. These real-time credit-push systems have quickly become part of the core payments systems in their countries.

New Rails: Open-Loop RTRP

Real-time retail payments (RTRP), sometimes called Faster Payments, are just what they sound like: real-time interoperable payments systems. **They work exclusively in push (credit transfer) mode.**

Confusion Alert

Many RTRP systems now support, or plan to support, Request to Pay (RtP) messaging. Some people refer to these as pull payments; in fact, they are nonfinancial messages that lead to push payments.

Most countries are developing single national platforms to handle RTRP systems. Others, notably the US, are enabling multiple systems.

These systems have in common their real-time nature; they also work on a continual (24/7/365) basis from the standpoint of both the paying and the receiving customer. Unlike ACH and checking systems, they are accompanied by a messaging layer that confirms to both payer and receiver that funds have been received.

Spotlight on Faster Payments

The UK's Faster Payments service was introduced in 2008 and has become something of a poster child for RTRP systems globally. It was developed at the demand of national regulators, and implemented collaboratively by the UK's large financial institutions. Today, it is broadly used for multiple use cases, and continues to add services that improve utility.

RTRP System Differences: Structure and Governance

Although all RTRP systems have fundamental similarities, they also differ in important ways. Some differences reflect the newness of these systems and may resolve in time, while others are likely to continue in the future.

Implementing a new RTRP system requires answering questions like these:

- **Who operates the platform?** This may be an existing or newly defined bank consortium, central bank, or commercial enterprise.

- **Is the system a single national platform, either provided or supported by the central bank?** Or is it one of many RTRP systems in the country? If the latter, is there intersystem connectivity?

- **Who writes the platform rules?** Can participating FSPs vote on these rules? Comment on them?

- **Interchange model?** Some systems have none; some have a "payer institution pays" or "payee institution pays" model. Others vary interchange by use case.

- **What types of institutions can participate?** In many markets, new non-bank FSPs are allowed to offer transaction accounts. Does the RTRP system connect only banks? Only non-bank FSPs? Both?

Spotlight on TIPS

The Central Bank of Tanzania is developing TIPS, an RTRP system that will connect both banks and non-bank e-money issuers in the country.

RTRP System Differences: Functional Capabilities

- **What type of messaging is used?** This topic has many layers; one is the structure of the payment messages. Many RTRP systems, particularly those owned by governments or bank associations, prefer the ISO 20022 message format, which has many subsets. More API-first systems use other protocols; the card networks, which have evolved to support RTRP payments ("pushing" transactions through their pull payment networks), use the older ISO 8583 format. And the large private-label RTRP systems (discussed below) have their own proprietary formats. Then there's API access itself. Is it defined by the scheme, by a government or quasi-government agency, or by individual FSP participants? Finally, the topic of end-user data carried with the RTRP system is complex. Some systems, particularly those geared to B2B transactions, are designed to carry invoice data; ISO20022 is structured to do this. Other systems, particularly those geared to P2P transactions, can carry consumer messaging ("here's my share of dinner"), and sometimes emojis, along with a payment.

- **How is interparticipant settlement managed?** The interparticipant settlement may be net deferred batch, net same-day batch, gross real-time, or continuous gross settlement.

Spotlight on the RTP Network

In 2018 in the US, The Clearing House introduced the RTP Network, which uses an innovative "continuous gross settlement" model. All participating banks share ownership of a single settlement account at the Federal Reserve Bank of New York. At any given point, a bank's share of that pooled account is defined by a position ledger kept by the system, eliminating the need for settlement windows or settlement entry posting.

- **What is the payments addressing model?** This model, critically, refers to how the payee, and the payee's FSP, identifies the recipient of a payment. There are a wide variety of models here, ranging from the simple (relies on the payer institution knowing the payee's account details) to flat directory models to broadcast models ("which FSP owns this address?"). More sophisticated systems support multiple address methodologies, each with its own resolution path; some systems require a payment address for both payer and payee.

In a push payments system, the "address" (payer identification) does not need to be secret or tokenized, as it cannot be used to pull money from the receiver's account. The exception is if an address is something (such as a bank account number) that can also be used in a pull payments system.

- **Will the system support Request to Pay (RtP) messaging?** RTRP systems work exclusively in push mode, but many are evolving to also support RtP messages—nonfinancial messages that flow from the payment acceptor (the merchant or biller, or its agent) to the payer, asking that money be pushed to the acceptor. There is debate whether RtP messages should be carried through the payments system or delivered outside it. If the latter, an RtP message can be a cross-payment-system message—an electronic invoice, in essence, that can be paid through not just an RTRP system, but other systems as well.

Another debate, when RtP is used with a single RTRP system, is whether or not a so-called "consumer mandate" may accompany a request to pay, giving the consumer's bank preauthorization to make a push payment without the consumer's involvement. (Interestingly, this makes a push payment look a lot like a pull payment.)

One possibility to consider here is that payer FSPs may create value-added "push-on-your-behalf" services for their customers, which would make RTRP payments look a lot like today's ACH direct debit payments. Adding to the complexity, some systems could support a "request to request to pay." For example, in a bill pay use case, a customer might send a message asking a biller "What do I owe you?" them make a full or partial payment. This would move the biller to send a "request to pay," which in turn would generate a push payment. Within this choice, of course, a number of design questions would need to be made.

RtP has existed for quite a while, in several forms. Notably, Brazil's **boleto system**, which started as a paper invoice payable by a consumer at a bank branch, has evolved to support digital delivery of both boleto and payment.

Challenge: To Overlay or Not to Overlay?

A much-debated term in the industry is "overlay," most often used in connection with RTRP systems. The general notion is a service that, as its name implies, rests on top of the RTRP rails. Although people agree on that definition, after that there are only questions and sharply contrasting opinions. Some believe that overlays are in some way part of, or sanctioned by, a specific payments system, but operate separately, with system participants opting in; the UK's Faster Payments system's Paym addressing directory overlay is an example. Others see overlays as purely commercial offerings that take advantage of, but are not part of, payments systems. Such overlays will work across multiple payments systems; the UKs approach to open banking is an example here.

- **Is there QR code support?** Many RTRP systems in the developing world are introducing QR code-enabled merchant payments. Merchants display a QR code that, when scanned by the consumer's phone, triggers a push payment over an RTRP system. In most instances, the QR code mechanism resembles an RtP message in that it results in the consumer sending a credit to the merchant. In more developed countries, where existing card networks are entrenched for merchant payments, this is less common; QR code or NFC payments are more likely to be implemented in connection with those networks.

- **What about cross-border RTRP payments?** Today, some ACH systems connect across borders, generally in credit-push mode. There is, of course, considerable demand for cross-border payments, and many fintechs addressing the opportunity. In theory, directly connecting national RTRP platforms would obviate the need for these services—but it's not at all clear how this segment of the industry will evolve.

Spotlight on Mojaloop

Mojaloop is an open-source software project designed to enable interoperable payments systems. It grew out of **The Level One Project,** an initiative of the Bill & Melinda Gates Foundation's Financial Services for the Poor group aimed at fostering inclusive interoperable payments systems. Mojaloop is based on open APIs originally developed by software companies supporting mobile wallets from e-money issuers. The software, and the specifications behind it, are highly secure and flexible, enabling transactions without the strong trust infrastructures of most incumbent systems. Mojaloop also notifies the paying customer of all payer and payee costs before approving a transfer. The Mojaloop open-source community is currently working on protocols to connect these systems cross-border, including pre-transfer notification of currency exchange costs.

New Rails: Closed-Loop RTRP

Most industry attention on faster payment rails focuses on interoperable (open-loop) RTRP systems. But there are also many large-scale closed-loop RTRP systems, most notably WeChat Pay and Alipay in China, and closed-loop mobile money operator services such as Kenya's M-PESA in Africa. These provide some end-user requirements of interoperable RTRP systems (real-time transfer, 24/7 operations, end-user notifications) but typically lack the ubiquity ("pay anyone") of interoperable systems.

Enhanced Rails

Many countries are also enhancing existing payments systems to make them more like RTRP systems:

- The huge ACH payments systems supporting the bulk of employer and government disbursements (payroll, benefits) and consumer bill payments (direct debits) in most developed countries are making changes to speed up batch processing. Often these changes include mandated end-of-day posting of funds to account holders.

Spotlight on Same-Day ACH

This US effort allows a batch of payments to be initiated and settled on the same day, rather than on the day after. This is still batch, not real-time, processing, but at a speed made possible by multiple settlement windows.

- FSP systems' settlement capabilities are being enhanced in several countries. The speed of settlement is increasing, and measures taken to reduce or eliminate liquidity risk.

Spotlight on SPEI

In Mexico, the central bank's wholesale RTGS system, SPEI, can now be used for low-value payments. A layer on top of SPEI, called CoDi, let's QR code and NFC payments use these rails. SPEI uses a near-gross settlement protocol for all transactions.

- Many countries are enhancing fraud control on domestic systems, including those used in cross-border transfers.

- Payments systems have traditionally been governed by system owners or participants—notably banks. In a few cases in the UK and Canada, governance (defined here as who sits on the board of the entity that writes scheme rules) is expanding to include a broader set of community stakeholders.

New Rails: Regional RTRP

Many regions are simultaneously introducing domestic RTRP systems and participating in their regional RTRP systems. These regional systems are designed for cross-border payments, though they may end up supporting domestic payments as well. Concentrating payment volumes in regional systems could dramatically lower processing costs and make operations and risk management more efficient; it would, however, require countries' central banks to cede some control. Regional initiatives that are operational or in development include SADC and TCIB (southern Africa), COMESA (eastern and central Africa), EAPS (eastern Africa), Mowali (Africa), SEPA Instant (Europe), BUNA (Middle East), and APN (Asia).

What Makes Innovation in Rails Successful?

In a word, **ubiquity**. Payments rails succeed when they connect large numbers of payers and payees—either through interoperability (most card systems and RTRP country rail systems) or market dominance (Kenya's M-PESA, China's WeChat Pay and Alipay).

Payments Innovations: Transaction Account Providers

TODAY'S FLOURISHING FINTECH LANDSCAPE is full of new provider types. Here we focus on **transaction account providers**—the entities holding payer or payee funds in some type of account. **Bank deposit accounts**, sometimes called **checking** or **current** accounts, are the most common—and least innovative. Many countries also allow entities such as saving institutions and credit unions to offer transaction accounts.

Confusion Alert

Two common terms are used very differently by different jurisdictions and providers.

Wallet can mean:

- A transaction account offered by an e-money issuer (defined below). The terms *e-money, e-money issuer,* and *e-money wallet* are used by both banks and licensed non-banks. In some jurisdictions, a bank might offer both a regular deposit account and an e-money account.

- Digital transaction initiation by a provider, such as Apple Pay, that neither holds nor moves funds.

- A service from a provider, such as PayPal, that sometimes holds, and sometimes simply moves, funds.

Payments service provider can mean:

- An e-money issuer.

- A money transmitter.

- A payments facilitator.

Glenbrook recommends focusing on the function of an enterprise or product, rather than its label.

The innovation here is regulatory expansion that offers transaction accounts to new categories of enterprises. In emerging economies, this helps reach unbanked people unserved by traditional banking models. In developed economies, it increases competition, enabling providers to offer less expensive, more innovative accounts and services.

- Some countries have recognized **new bank types.** A new class of banks in India, *payments banks*, can open accounts, but not engage in lending or other banking activities. In other markets, microfinance institutions can hold customer funds in accounts under special charter arrangements, though not all do.

- Many countries recognize the role of **e-money issuer**, a new category of transaction account provider. National regulations specify which enterprises can offer such accounts; in many African countries, for example, mobile network operators can do so by chartering a separate business entity. The thinking is that these companies already have digital relationships with unbanked people—for example, through mobile phone accounts. Their agent networks, which enroll customers in phone services and accept cash "top-ups" to mobile accounts, can perform similar functions for e-money accounts.

Spotlight on M-PESA

Kenya's M-PESA has a well-deserved position as poster child for e-money issuance. The company has 22.6 million accounts serving a country with an adult population of 29 million; some reports PIN transaction volume at nearly 50% of GDP. Near-dominance of the underlying mobile phone network means no interoperability demands. M-PESA has partnered with banks to offer P2P, merchant, and bill payments, as well as microlending and savings products.

It's Not Just Kenya: GSMA, the mobile network operator industry association, produces an annual report on the state of the mobile money industry. Its 2019 report counts 272 mobile money deployments in 90 countries.

- E-money in a customer's account is an obligation of the issuer to that customer, much like money in a bank account. But where a bank needs to keep only a small percentage of these funds at the central bank (the reserve requirement), e-money issuers must keep 100% of customer funds in one or more commercial bank accounts, called trust deposits. Regulation can be quite specific about controls necessary to ensure that trust deposits exactly match the amount the issuer has in customer accounts. Such accounts are denominated in the fiat currency of the country and meant to be spendable like fiat currency.

The E-Money Trap:

- Defining "e-money" as different than "money" raises questions about interoperability. Can a payments system exchange payments between bank accounts and e-money accounts? If an employer wants to pay salaries into e-money accounts, must it first "buy" e-money? Regulators are slowly sorting out such questions. Note, however, that where non-banks are permitted to open transaction accounts in partnership with banks, this problem does not exist. How different, really, is a partner-bank program from e-money issuance with trust deposits in a bank?

- E-money wallets charge a fee to the sender and a fee to the recipient when "cashing out"; the e-money issuer pays an agent commission on each side of the transaction. One can argue that issuers make most of their revenue from cash-out fees. What happens to this business model as merchant acceptance of digital payments increases and people cash out less frequently?

- National regulations may permit, or even mandate, **agents** to represent banks and/or e-money issuers. Agents generally accept deposits and manage withdrawals (called "cash-in/cash-out in e-money countries). Agents may be exclusive to an account provider, or represent multiple providers; some countries have agent networks managed by management companies. The complex economics of agents may either help or hinder national goals encouraging digital transactions.

- Many countries permit, with or without explicit regulation, non-bank enterprises to offer **general-purpose store-of-value accounts** in partnership with banks. In such prepaid card programs, a commercial entity such as a store provides the card, which is a transaction account holding customer funds. The money is kept in a commercial bank partnered with the card. While this is much like e-money, the funds are defined not as such, but simply as the obligation of the partner bank to the end customer. Typically, the partner bank is a member of a debit or credit card network, and the payment card can be used to make payments anywhere its network brand is accepted.

Spotlight on Direct Express

In the United States, the highly successful Direct Express program provides a prepaid government benefits card that can be used to store funds, make purchases, and pay bills. The program permits one free ATM withdrawal per deposit received.

- Particularly in the developed world, many "challenger banks" are taking a digital-first, and often digital-only, approach to consumer transaction accounts. Many of these banks struggle to reach a critical customer mass, and to make their business models profitable. Some are front-end services layered on top of actual bank accounts provided by a partner bank; others have bank charters in their jurisdiction. Some, like Chime in the US, rely primarily on interchange and interest income on deposits received; others, such as Monzo in the UK and N26 in Germany, include some element of lending in their business models.

- **Private store-of-value accounts** offered by non-banks: Funds in these accounts are often restricted in use. Examples are single-store gift cards and mobile payments apps, like those from Starbucks.

Spotlight on Starbucks

Starbucks has a very popular private store-of-value account used with a card or mobile app. By encouraging customers to fund their wallets (from a bank account or credit card) once with enough money to cover multiple purchases, Starbucks lowers its total per-transaction fees. This is a particularly good model for a company with many frequent customers and low-value transactions. At one point, Starbucks claimed to be the "largest mobile payment system in the world."

What Makes Transaction Account Providers' Innovations Successful?

Authorizing non-banks to provide transaction accounts appears to be most successful where those enterprises already have significant customer bases with digital relationships, as with African e-money issuers that are, or are affiliated with, mobile network operators. These non-banks also need an achievable business model. The spotty record of India's payments banks can be attributed to business model issues, perhaps due to legal limits on their activities.

Payments Innovations: Products and Services

THESE INNOVATIVE PRODUCTS AND services use the payments rails and transaction account providers described above.

Access Innovations

Arguably the most visible payments innovations, these let consumers, merchants, billers, enterprises, and other end users initiate or receive payments via existing rails and transaction accounts.

Access Innovation: Modes of Access

Card-centric developed economies play host to many new methods of physically initiating or receiving card payments, often referred to as *proximity payments*. These use existing rails and transaction accounts, but are often enabled by tech innovations requiring scheme rule changes.

- **New access modes for initiating card payments:** Global introduction of both contact and contactless chip cards is one example of a "sustaining innovation" that strengthens existing products and services. The use of QR codes to effect card payments, in either consumer-presented or merchant-presented modes, is another.

- **New access modes for receiving card payments:** An example here is mobile acceptance technologies that let merchants accept card payments by phone rather than card terminal, via technologies such as QR codes, NFC, and audio-jack "dongles."

- **New access modes for RTRP payments:** In markets without established card industries, innovation can enable whole new ecosystems. Where e-money can be issued, for example, consumers can use USSD channels to initiate payments by phone. In Nigeria, many providers use a traditional POS to string together a series of USSD codes, effecting push payments for purchases and transfers. And in China and elsewhere, QR codes, most often in the merchant-presented mode, have been the defining factor in rapid adoption of mobile-initiated payments. In China, these payments run over the proprietary closed-loop rails of the two dominant providers—Alipay and WeChat Pay—and are eventually funded by draws on consumers' bank accounts.

Organizer wallets: We've discussed how the term "wallet" is used to describe a confusing number of functional payments approaches. We are coining the term *organizer wallet* to describe a product that lets consumers initiate payment transactions, where the wallet provider does not actually move money or provide transaction accounts. Typically, organizer wallets let consumers store multiple cards (and sometimes, other payments methods), choosing from them at the time of payment.

Most of the activity we note in this category is in card-centric developed markets. It's important here to distinguish purchases made in the POS domain (sometimes called *proximity payments*) from purchases in the Remote Commerce domain.

- **In the POS domain,** Apple Pay is an example of an organizer wallet. Consumers use it to initiate card transactions, but it provides no consumer or merchant transaction accounts. It uses no card rails; they're used by the card issuer and the merchant acquirer. Like competitors Samsung Pay and Google Pay, Apple Pay uses a combination of NFC (or NFC-like) technologies and tokenization to secure the account number. These services are covered under card scheme rules, and in general result in transactions with a merchant-favorable card-present status.

- **In the Remote Commerce domain,** card networks and financial institutions have offered multiple waves of organizer wallets, facilitating card-not-present transactions, with rules less favorable to merchants than card-present transactions. None achieved substantial penetration. In 2019, joint specifications developed by EMVCo, called **Secure Remote Commerce** (SRC), standardized ecommerce transaction processing across remote-checkout environments. The resulting transactions still have card-not-present status.

Caveat: Other ecommerce wallet companies, such as PayPal, are described later, as over-the-top players.

- A new term in online and mobile commerce is **in-app payments.** These may be payments within a proprietary merchant wallet, or the wallet of an over-the-top player, made with a card on file. They can also be made remotely through an organizer wallet such as Apple Pay. In either case, if the card credential is tokenized, the transaction may have card-present status.

Complication

Mobile iOS apps that embed digital content purchases have to pay 30% to Apple—the percentage app developers pay for app sales. Music, ebooks, movies, and more are subject to this constraint. Unsurprisingly, many vendors ask purchasers to buy digital content via browser links. This fee doesn't apply to purchase of physical goods (for delivery) through iOS apps.

What's happening with access modes for remote purchase in emerging economies? It's not clear yet. Every payments system operator has the capability, or a plan, to enable remote purchases. But what rules apply (card-present equivalent?) is rarely clear, and the notion of an organizer wallet is not broadly seen.

Access Innovation: Third-Party Payment Initiation

In legacy interoperable payments systems of all kinds, system rules allow only one participating FSP to initiate a payment. (If the paying FSP initiates, it is a push payment; if the payee initiates it, it is a pull payment.) A third party may physically initiate a payment, but always on behalf of an FSP—which remains responsible, from a rules and settlement perspective, for the transaction.

We're seeing radical innovation in this area, with some regulatory jurisdictions and payments systems permitting **third-party payment initiation**—part of what's referred to as **open banking**.

Confusion Alert

The term *open banking* is used for two different activities: one giving non-banks access to bank data, and the other allowing non-banks (or, to be precise, FSPs that don't provide transaction accounts) to initiate payments transactions. We're discussing the second here.

There are two approaches to third-party payment initiation. The first is driven by regulators and applies across payments systems; examples include the EU's PSD2 (Payment Services Directive 2) and the UK's Open Banking protocol (set up by the UK Competition and Markets Authority). In the UK, a registered payment initiation services provider (PISP) can, with the consumer's consent, connect via API to the consumer's bank or other account-holding FSP and create a transaction through Faster Payments, the UK's RTRP system. While the consumer's bank still authenticates the PIN and verifies fund availability, the PISP creates the transaction—the bank has no choice but to accept it. The UK protocol could be used in a similar way to make a card payment.

The other approach is system-specific, with the rules of a particular system permitting third-party initiation. (India's UPI is an example here.) A broad generalization: The cross-system approach could inspire more long-term end-user participation, while the single-system approach may show more rapid short-term growth.

An interesting consequence of introducing PISPs is that both sender and receiver need payment addresses. In a traditional interoperable RTRP system, only the receiver needs an address.

Access Innovation: APIs

The use of APIs to access digital services of all kinds is of course widespread, with significant and growing impact on payments. Increasingly, APIs are how financial institutions connect to payments schemes, to each other, to customers, and to partners. There are several different types of financial APIs:

- The earliest use of APIs in financial services was a simple efficiency play that gave financial institutions' customers an additional way to access existing data platforms and services. These APIs were generally proprietary and often cumbersome; one bank's first API user guide was a 300-page PDF!

- A newer generation of software applications are built as "API-first" designs. In the short term, this simply means easier-to-use, and therefore more productive, APIs. Over time, however, it has the potential to transform the industry, replacing a traditional hub-and-spoke architecture with a mesh of interacting systems and system components—think "the internet of things meets payments." Imagine, for example, a digital payment order that, instead of relying on rules written by a scheme-controlled hub, carries its own instructions: "If you accept this transaction, you will settle it like this, at this cost ...."

- Today, APIs are how open banking works. Many fintechs, able to access payments systems in new, more direct ways because of law and regulation or private system operating rules, do so with APIs. In the European Economic Area, the PSD2 regulation requires banks to use APIs to make their systems available to registered AISPs (account information service providers) and PISPs (payment initiation service providers).

Security Innovations

Payments security is a fundamental requirement for digital systems. The global card industry was an early advocate for, and pioneer in, the development of solutions to payments fraud. Today's four most significant security innovations:

- **Tokenization:** The relatively simple process of swapping out a "real" payment credential for a limited-purpose token effectively reduces theft of pull payment credentials (and subsequent criminal use), offering a solution for card data breaches. As noted above, in push payments systems, if the payee's payment address is an alias, or anything that can't be used in a pull payments system, the question of tokenization is moot.

- **Biometrics:** After years of small-scale efforts, the use of biometrics in payments is growing—especially in emerging economies, many of which use biometrically authenticated national identities. The success of these programs is driven by regulation, in India with Aadhaar, and in other countries where regulators tie biometric authentication to SIM card registration. Fingerprint and facial recognition, becoming common on smartphones, are now carrying over to laptops and other devices.

As the use of **digital identification** grows, there is no consensus on which entities should issue or control IDs. Fintechs such as GlobalID continue to pursue the concept of private digital identity, separate from state or sovereign identities.

- **Digital signatures:** This technology, fundamental to the internet for 20 years, is finding new uses in payments. Digitally signed messaging between financial institutions and payments hubs can, at some levels, replace the security architectures of legacy payments systems, which depend on heavily secured channels controlled by systems or hubs. Interestingly, cross-border payments—which by definition involve at least two separate transactions in two country systems, can, using these technologies, "lock" two transactions, completing each only if the other happens. Ripple, the Interledger Protocol, and Mojaloop are all pursuing such "atomic" transactions.

- **Device recognition and geolocation:** With smartphone payment initiation now common, adding device recognition to personal authentication strengthens security. Geolocation technologies also strengthen fraud detection, particularly for merchant payments.

Spotlight on Apple Pay

Apple Pay security technology includes tokenization, biometrics, device recognition, and digital signatures.

Payments Optimization Innovation

The payments landscape has always included processors—service firms that banks, merchants, and payments networks outsource various functions to. In recent years, innovative forms of processing have emerged, helping payments acceptors (merchants, billers, and other enterprises) deal with the rise in "alternative payments solutions." That complexity extends to payments system rules and routing options and, particularly for remote-commerce merchants, the desire to expand into global markets.

We call these processors *payments optimizers*, as they specialize in helping payments acceptors simplify their payments options. They're also called PSPs (payments services providers), GPSPs (global payments services providers), or simply gateways.

Confusion Alert

Add *gateway* to the list of confusing payment terms. While it often describes a payment optimizer, it can also refer to an entity that converts data formats (between payments systems, for example). In some emerging countries, national RTRP systems are referred to as gateways. So be careful—don't assume a universal definition.

A few payments optimizers provide end-customer services as over-the-top players. Some play the role of card acquirer or money transmitter, and several offer fraud protection and regulatory compliance services. These firms usually have highly flexible service offerings for merchant customers. A large merchant might use its services to handle a particular alternative payment product, or to enter a new global marketplace. The largest often bring these functions in house once they've reached a certain point of maturity.

Some payments optimizers start from relatively small niches. For example, **Yapily** helps customers connect to bank APIs; UK regulations require the nine largest banks to make API access available, though each may have a slightly different API. And **Hover** is helping firms in Africa connect Android app developers to mobile money operators' USSD menus.

A number of firms have tried to apply this concept to consumer payments, with little success. In the US, for example, **Coin** (now closed) introduced a card that customers could load multiple card data onto. The idea was that the consumer could then choose, or be helped to choose, the best payment option for a given purchase. Others including **Fuze**, **Stratos**, **Plastc**, and **Swyp** tried similar approaches.

Business Model Innovations

Some of them most interesting adaptations in payments products and services have been to providers' business models.

- Revenue model innovations tend to use what economists call "adjacencies" rather than payments transaction fees. This is actually not that new in banking. Banks have historically used the value of transaction account balances, and more significantly lending, as a source of revenue, reducing the need to charge for transactions. Initially, the card acceptance industry focused on transaction revenue in developed economies. But in emerging economies trying to bring small and poor merchants into the digital payments space, many providers have turned to lending as the "adjacency" that can best support digital merchant payments.

- Many companies are using consumer transaction data—particularly from digital payments—to create a history on which to base credit decisions. This is an appealing alternative in markets where there are no credit bureaus, or where populations are not well represented in those bureaus. Just a few of these companies: **Lidya, Tala, Branch, M-Shwari, Upstart, Meritize,** and **Petal.**

- While countries in Latin America have allowed installment purchases for many years, financed by either card issuers or merchants, larger developed economies are seeing a new wave of installment lending, facilitated by technology from companies such as **Klarna, Affirm, Bread, Afterpay,** and **SplitIt.**

- Some **commerce platforms** are taking "adjacencies" to an extreme. Rather than gaining revenue from transactions or related financial services, a platform's business model may revolve around the margin on the sale of goods and services—with payments services simply an enabling component in its closed-loop payments system. Such business models often mix transaction-related revenue and commerce margins. The Chinese duopoly of **WeChat Pay** and **Alipay** are examples (when seen as components of their "super-apps"), as are ride-sharing platforms such as **Grab** and multiproduct platforms such as **Rappi.**

- About 15 years ago, the card industry formalized what is now known as the **payment facilitator model,** in which enterprises accept payments on behalf of smaller merchants. PayPal pioneered this model for online commerce, as did Square for in-person commerce. **BSA's TCIB** (transactions cleared on an immediate basis) system uses a similar model in southern Africa, including system "hubs," each with a cluster of customers either sending or receiving funds. The innovation here is to the cost model. In the card industry, for example, rather than requiring lengthy and expensive onboarding of individual merchants, the facilitator can rapidly and inexpensively onboard groups—while retaining liability exposure for the underlying companies.

> **E-money issuance,** described earlier, is another radical business model innovation, replacing the costly concept of branch banking with the vastly more cost-efficient mobile money paradigm.

What Makes Product and Service Innovations Successful?

At Glenbrook, we find it useful to distinguish between **unilateral innovations**, which can be adopted independently by one side of a payment transaction, and **multilateral innovations**, which require two (or more) parties in a transaction to adopt the desired change. Unilateral innovations are easier to launch, but multilateral innovations have more potential to scale. This is the primary factor we use to assess the success of product and service innovations.

> **Introduction of chip cards** in an already card-enabled market is a classic example of multilateral innovation. To put it in place, new cards need to be issued, new terminals and ATMs provisioned, and processor and network capabilities updated.

- **Access innovations** are typically multilateral, and require industry (and often national) agreement and collaboration to be put in effect. The UK's adoption of chip-and-PIN technology is a classic success story of national regulators and financial providers collaborating on rapid adoption of a new access mode. India's success with UPI is another example. Access innovations are occasionally unilateral—for example, using a smartphone dongle to accept card payments.

- **Security innovations** are also most likely to succeed when introduced collaboratively—card issuer tokenization is an example. The use of biometrics for payments security may be the result of a commitment to national IDs, as with Pakistan's adoption of biometric SIM registration, which was then used to secure over-the-counter mobile money transfers. Biometrics may also be introduced unilaterally; Apple Pay, for example uses the fingerprint and facial recognition capabilities of Apple device hardware.

- **Payments optimization innovations,** as services provided to individual merchants or payments acceptors, are unilateral almost by definition. Success has generally been defined by a solution's ease of use and number of integrated payment options.

- **Business model innovations** are often unilateral. Regulatory changes that, for example, enable new categories of lender or (as with e-money) transaction account providers can inspire these innovations.

Payments Innovations: Over-the-Top and Out-of-the-Box Innovations

SO FAR WE'VE DISCUSSED innovation in payments rails, transaction account providers, and products and services. Now we look at **over-the-top** and **out-of-the-box** innovations, which have drawn the bulk of high-level investment in payments.

Over-the-Top Innovations

In this category we include fintechs, businesses that create products and services that sit on top of, and use, core payments systems. These are not simple organizer wallets, but financial intermediaries that take control of the flow of funds. At its simplest, an over-the-top business might accept payment into its own bank account from a payer, then disburse funds from there to a payee.

This model supports transaction processing, which at Glenbrook we often refer to as "decoupled." In decoupled transactions, the two (or more) parts of a transaction may be physically separate, with a provider using one payments system and receiving bank account for the first half of the transaction, and another payments system and disbursing account for the second half. This gives providers a high degree of flexibility, and allows arbitrage of cost, timing, and risk differences in the two systems.

Technically, all cross-border payments follow this model—receipt of payment in the payments system in the sending country is half of the transaction, and disbursement of payment in the payments system in the receiving country the other half. This is true in both traditional correspondent-banking-enabled cross border transfers and the money transmitter remittance model. Though we may not think of this funds intermediation model as inventive, innovative fintechs are embracing and building on it in new and creative ways.

We see two categories of notable innovation here, the money transmitter and account wallet models.

The Money Transmitter Model

As mentioned above, all money transmitters use a financial intermediation model. But innovative approaches are transforming aspects of cross-border remittance and domestic payments in some countries.

Some players use available internet and smartphone technologies to make much more information available to end users—increasing transparency, particularly with respect to fees, in traditionally opaque marketplaces.

Other players take advantage of the ubiquitous use of card payments in some countries to create the effect of a single transfer using a decoupled model.

Spotlight on TransferWise

*TransferWise's cross-border remittance service shows the sending customer all elements of the fees they will pay—and compares its foreign exchange rate to market benchmarks and competitive rates, even when its own rates are less advantageous. The company capitalizes on open banking and other enabling regulation to become a direct settling participant in the UK's Faster Payments system. There are many other players, new and old, following this space, including **Revolut, OFX, Western Union, Remitly** and **Xoom** (PayPal).*

Spotlight on Square's Cash App

This app takes advantage of the fact that in the US, all banked customers have debit cards. Once a payer and payee have registered on the app, the payer can transfer funds immediately. What's happening "under the hood": Square, acting as a merchant, pulls funds from the payer's debit card account and deposits them into its own bank account. Then, acting as a paying financial institution, it immediately pushes funds (over the same or a different card network) out of its own account and into the payee's debit card account. Of course, during this process Square is also updating the payer and payee's accounts on its own closed-loop books.

The Account Wallet Model

We've described confusion around the term *wallet*, and introduced the term *organizer wallet* to describe a provider that doesn't touch funds, but rather offers a payer the ability to choose from multiple payments cards or instruments. Here we discuss another use of the term, which we will call the **account wallet**. An account wallet provider keeps a private account (not a bank account) or ledger on its books to record deposits and disbursements of funds for an individual consumer or merchant. Technically, this makes it a closed-loop payments system operator. The provider then enables its customers to use these funds to pay each other. From a regulatory point of view, account wallet providers are required to hold 100% of the funds at a commercial bank.

Confusion Alert

We distinguish the account wallet model from e-money issuers, which are enabled by regulation as transaction account providers; most regulators expect these entities to become participants in interoperable RTRP systems in their countries. Account wallet providers rely on these interoperable payments systems for deposits into, and disbursements out of, their private closed-loop wallets.

Spotlight on PayPal

PayPal arguably defined this model in its early incarnations in the US marketplace. Consumers and merchants open accounts on PayPal's books; the money is deposited in aggregate in commercial bank(s). Payments from one customer to another are simply recorded on PayPal's books. PayPal then uses card, ACH, RTRP, and other payments systems to fund consumers' accounts, and disburses funds, when requested, out of the merchant's accounts. Note that PayPal has evolved from its original model, with variants in place in the US and in global markets where the company is active.

Aggregators

Spotlight on China

WeChat Pay started as a social platform and Alipay as an ecommerce payment player, but the two have arrived at very similar positions. They offer customers and merchants account wallets used to effect payments. Accounts are funded, for consumers, and distributed, for merchants, on an occasional basis, using China's interoperable IBPS payments system.

In many markets, players have emerged to help in the growth of digital payments systems. An aggregator will often focus first on a single use case, helping kick-start use of a payments system by working to sign up individual end customers; it may also support data integration requirements. A bill pay aggregator may sign up a number of billers in a country, along with consumers who want to make payments. Aggregators are typically payments-system agnostic, allowing customers to pay, for example, with a mobile money wallet app. The funds go into the aggregator's bank account, then the aggregator disburses them to the biller. This intermediation becomes unnecessary once both consumer and biller have accounts on an RTRP system, but aggregators will probably continue to provide value in end-user sign up and data integration.

> The fintech universe is full of businesses that are not payments companies but are enabled by digital payments. A working-capital loan company, for example, may depend on deductions from sales for loan repayments. A consumer insurance company might replace quarterly bills with smaller, more regular digital payments. And then there's Netflix and a raft of other subscription services.

Out-of-the-Box Innovations

We've talked about transaction accounts, and digital payments made out of or into those accounts. The innovation has been in who provides these accounts, the payments systems built to work with them, and the products and services layered on top of them.

Out-of-the-box innovation simply replaces all of that. It will not surprise you to read that this is the territory of cryptocurrencies. The crypto world also includes users of blockchain and related technologies; many of these are incremental improvements on secured databases, and not truly innovative. But true cryptocurrencies are new and different, with an intent to replace transaction accounts as we know them along with the associated payments systems.

Cryptocurrencies

Cryptocurrencies do not use transaction accounts. A ledger records them, and "wallets" (another use of that term!) are used to manage them. But the cryptocurrencies within are not the obligation of the wallet provider, or of another financial institution. In an oft-used metaphor, they're more like what's in your safety deposit box than what's in your bank account.

Since Bitcoin was introduced in 2008, the financial services industry and its customers have learned a lot:

- It's not easy to get a new payments system going—you need a critical mass of both payers and payees. This has historically been the great pain point of any new payments system, and crypto is no different.

- Customers have the same user requirements for crypto as for any other payments system: usability, security, affordability, ubiquity. There are customer niches that care about one particular attribute (in the case of crypto, anonymity—particularly for criminal users), but this doesn't scale.

- If customers are going to convert cryptocurrencies into their own (fiat) currencies, existing foreign exchange mechanisms (brokers, exchanges, etc.) work just fine.

- Cryptocurrency raises well-documented (and incredibly complex) technical hurdles. There are multiple solution approaches, none of which has gained overall market acceptance. The resulting disarray creates uncertainty and hinders adoption.

- It isn't simple to get to a lower-cost solution than today's large-scale mainstream payments systems. In the early days of Bitcoin, much was made of the potential for merchant costs to be lower than those for card acceptance. But the cost of card and RTRP acceptance is trending down, and the cost of cryptocurrencies is higher than originally perceived.

- Very real concern about stability has inspired several "stable coin" offerings that seek to minimize the volatility of digital assets. These concepts, and the companies using them, are quite new.

- Cryptocurrency regulation is still in its infancy. The leading edge is home to uncertainty—and sometimes regulatory problems (and fines!) when companies find themselves outside of regulations.

Perhaps the best way to think of cryptocurrencies today is as a slow-burning fire. It hasn't gotten all that big, despite occasional flares. But it hasn't been put out yet, either, and in places around the world where fiat currencies are weak, or among people who care about anonymity, it has found a home. Economies that falter due to crises such as the current pandemic are likely to see those flames grow.

Spotlight on Libra

The stable coin currency announced by Facebook and its partners in 2019 has been met with widespread skepticism in the financial services industry, most of it centered around regulatory uncertainty, and the consortium is now pivoting to be more compliant with global regulations. Skepticism is understandable—but keep in mind the model of WeChat Pay in China, where another mammoth social media platform created what is now one of two dominant retail payments systems.

Digital Fiat Currencies

What are digital fiat currencies? Right now, there's little agreement other than what the term implies—some kind of digital payments delivery sanctioned by a national government. At least two very different approaches are under discussion:

- **Account-based ledger systems** using blockchain technologies to secure the record of funds held. Think of this as a version of an RTGS wire transfer system, with applicability for wholesale payments. These systems would not necessarily hold cryptocurrencies, and arguably are no more "digital" than existing RTGS or RTRP systems. In some such systems, consumers might hold accounts directly at the central bank—a regulatory change highly disruptive to a country's banks, whose economic models depend on their customer deposit base.

- **Token-based systems** that have the central bank of a country issuing crypto tokens, either directly to consumers or distributed in some fashion through banks. These approaches attempt to mimic some of the appeal of cash, although their use, if it became popular, would be unlikely to be restricted to today's cash users.

> **Spotlight on China:** China has signaled intent to issue a national fiat currency. What this looks like, and how it works, will greatly affect development of this sector.

Success Factors in Over-the-Top and Out-of-the-Box Innovations

Over-the-Top Innovations

Over-the-top players succeed through creativity. This might mean thinking creatively about how to use payments systems, sometimes in ways unintended by their operators. PayPal's original payments facilitator model, for example, famously went against Visa and Mastercard's rules at the time. Successful players in these categories have focused relentlessly on end-user adoption, and have been willing to pivot their business and processing models to gain traction.

Out-of-the-Box Innovations

One can argue that no company has yet achieved success with an out-of-the-box approach. A successful out-of-the-box play would need both a critical mass of customers and regulatory support.

The Innovation Imperative for Financial Inclusion

What is Financial Inclusion?

Throughout the world, in both emerging and developed economies, substantial numbers of people are excluded from the formal financial economy. This means that they have no transaction accounts in which to safely keep funds, and cannot participate in payments and other financial services connected to those accounts. The excluded are overwhelmingly the working poor and most vulnerable—large populations in emerging economies, but also the poor in developed economies. Many governments have financial inclusion strategies designed to benefit this target population and improve their countries' economic ecosystems.

Digital payments, and the transaction accounts that support them, are a defining element of financial inclusion and the enabling mechanism for many of its benefits.

> As this book is being written, the world is starting to come to grips with profound changes resulting from the **coronavirus pandemic.** Most estimates indicate deep economic damage to poor countries and poor people everywhere, with many previously employed people joining the ranks of the poor. Affordability, security, and reliability of payments will be paramount. To deliver benefits to the poor more efficiently and without costs and risks associated with physical delivery, digital payments will become an imperative.

Benefits of Financial Inclusion

Financial inclusion has myriad, well-documented benefits:

Consumer Financial Health

- **Transaction accounts** and the ability to make and receive payments let consumers safeguard funds and control their financial positions.

- **Individual (vs. family) transaction accounts** give women in particular more opportunity to safeguard funds and control disbursement. Research also shows that women, given control over payments, are more likely to spend on critical services for the family such as healthcare and school fees.

- **Savings accounts** help consumers weather financial shocks and build a digital financial history that can be the basis for securing loans. Consumers can build for their futures with targeted short- and long-term savings programs, and make payments on insurance policies to further safeguard their interests.

- **All consumers** can better participate in the "digital mainstream," including use of online government and school services.

> It's not just government working to overcome the challenges of the unbanked. A broad global community of organizations, including development banks, private foundations and development organizations, industry associations, and businesses are working with governments to promote and enable financial inclusion.

Governments and Businesses

- **Governments, nonprofits, and businesses** that disburse funds can do so directly, bypassing intermediaries. This can get disbursements to beneficiaries faster, and reduce graft and leakage associated with cash handling.

- **Small businesses** can pay for goods and services electronically, improving their ability to control cash flow and match it to incoming funds. Businesses can also build a digital financial history to support borrowing.

- **Commercial providers** have found new businesses (and new business models!) serving previously excluded populations.

The Economy

- **Inclusive economies** are prosperous economies. Digital financial services let more people participate in the financial ecosystem.

- **Tax authorities** can collect taxes from many more businesses. Depending on country policies, digital financial services could incentivize small businesses to transition from the informal to the formal economy.

A 2016 McKinsey study indicated that widespread use of digital finance could boost the total annual GDP of emerging economies by $3.7 trillion by 2025, a 6% increase over a business-as-usual scenario.

Realizing the Goals of Financial Inclusion

What does it take to accomplish the goals of financial inclusion? Quite a lot, as it turns out. No single "silver bullet" can turn a cash economy into a digital one.

What is clear is that innovation is a necessity. After all, very few people *choose* to be financially excluded; rather, they're excluded because financial services are either unavailable to them or too expensive or difficult to use. We discuss payments-related innovations in this section, many of them current or possible enablers of financial inclusion.

Enabling Policies

- **New types of account providers:** Many countries, finding that traditional commercial banks cannot—or will not—serve the poor, have enabled new classes of transaction account providers. These could be incumbents in other sectors, such as mobile network operators, or new classes of chartered banks.

- **Digital identity and KYC:** Opening a transaction account usually requires proof of identity, and lack of a solid national identity system is a barrier. Many countries are working on issuing biometric IDs that can be used for account opening and other financial processes. In the meantime, governments are developing ways to identify customers in the absence of foundational ID. The gold standard for inclusion is tiered KYC (know your customer) policies that let low-income people open limited-use transaction accounts with little or no formal proof of identity.

- **Payments business models** in developed countries are often driven by a combination of merchant acceptance fees and consumer lending fees; these are far less applicable in countries with large poor populations. Business models focusing instead on SME lending, data aggregation, or commerce platforms are more feasible, though they demand regulatory support.

Infrastructure

- **Interoperable digital payments systems:** Exchanging digital transactions requires interoperable real-time retail payments. Developing interoperable systems, which connect not only banks but also non-bank financial institutions, is a priority in many emerging economies. (Note that closed-loop systems, where dominant, can have the same effect, as with Kenya's M-PESA and China's WeChat Pay and Alipay duopoly.)

> ### Challenge
>
> Interoperable payments systems can't just connect poor people to each other; they need to enable payments among and between e-money wallets (if those exist in a country) and more traditional bank accounts. After all, poor people pay rich people and businesses, schools, and utility companies, and rich people and businesses pay poor people.

- **Merchant acceptance:** Making digital money "spendable" (at merchants, but also for bill payment and government payments) appears critical to motivate digital liquidity and break the cash-in/cash-out cycle. The good news here is that simple QR code-enabled merchant payments are much easier to get going than terminal-oriented acceptance systems. They can be especially useful in reaching remote locations and remaining affordable to small merchants. The limiting factor today is in areas with a lack of widespread or affordable data.

- **High volumes:** In a frustratingly circular manner, a payments system needs high enough volumes to have low enough unit costs to permit low-to-zero transaction pricing.

- **Security:** Obviously, consumers and merchants must have faith in the security of their funds in accounts and during transactions. This is especially important when introducing new payment types to customers with low levels of trust and familiarity in such offerings. Some countries with widely implemented biometric digital ID use these technologies for account opening and higher-value transactions.

Products and Services

- **Transaction accounts:** The cornerstone of financial inclusion is access to transaction accounts. Bank accounts, mobile money, specialty prepaid cards, or microfinance accounts can all safely hold money and enable payments to and from other accounts.

- **Agent-assisted cash-in/cash-out:** People living in a cash economy won't transition immediately to an all-electronic world; their transaction accounts and services must also work with cash, through branches, bank agents, ATMs, or mobile money agents. The economics of cash-in/cash-out (those agents need to be paid!) is a major challenge in financial inclusion. The end goal is to have people leave their money in digital form, and spend it digitally—a state some call "digital liquidity."

- **Ease of use:** A critical threshold for frequent use of digital accounts is ease of use, a factor often underestimated by new entrants. China's success with QR codes for merchant payments is notable here.

- **Affordable pricing**: Consumers and businesses look at payments costs through a use-case lens. A consumer willing to pay a fee to send a remittance (which would otherwise have a more expensive or risky path) will probably not be as willing to pay a fee to buy a loaf of bread. Merchants are less likely to adopt methods with associated fees if they see the cash alternative as free. Some governments are setting limits (as low as zero) on digital payments costs for merchants or end users.

Spotlight on China

In China, even very small and poor merchants, such as food stall operators and sidewalk vendors, can create QR codes on their smartphones, which they link to wallets and bank accounts. Of course, this assumes smartphones and bank accounts; not all countries have the same profile.

Why Innovation is Required

Ask "why are people financially excluded?" and you'll get many answers. Legacy transaction account models; the technical capabilities of FSPs, consumers, and enterprises; and legacy payments systems fail to provide the foundations. Our framework for payments innovations shows that innovations in all of these categories are necessary for financial inclusion.

The good news is that many building blocks are being put in place—but adoption is still slow. This author believes that, of all the many reasons, the biggest is the constraints of commercial business models. Perhaps as a consequence, many countries in the developing world are taking steps to define a national payments ecosystem as a public good.

Three Big Questions

NO ONE KNOWS THE future of global payments. But its trajectory depends in large part on the answers to three key questions:

1. **Should payments systems be viewed as infrastructure, or as a competitive marketplace?** Some regulators are beginning to talk about payments systems as public goods, akin to national highway systems or the internet's DNS. This argues for fewer, larger payments systems with universal attributes; products and services layered on that infrastructure would be the competitive arena. Other countries, especially those adopting RTRP systems, see competitive core payments systems as a better approach. Some, like the US, are planning multiple systems; others, like the UK, are focusing on single systems. The possible introduction of digital fiat currency in a country is an important factor here.

2. **How will open banking evolve?** If third-party initiators become the standard for retail payments, there will be a big divide between banks and other transaction account providers, and payments solutions providers that cause money to be moved. Do banks risk becoming dumb pipes if solution providers own more of the customer relationship?

3. **How will retail payments fraud be managed?** The global card industry has perfected a model for fraud management that, among other things, protects the consumer from bad-actor fraud by merchants and other payment acceptors. This model works well but is very expensive, with the burden on the FSP representing the merchant; that FSP must charge enough for payments acceptance to cover its liability. This model is unlikely to succeed in emerging markets with large populations of poor consumers and merchants. Alternative approaches are discussed, but a successful model has not yet emerged. This problem must be solved before digital payments can move into the larger global market.

What do you think? The Glenbrook team is always interested in your views on the global payments landscape, today and in the future. Direct your questions to books@glenbrook.com.

Index

Want to learn more about payments? Glenbrook's Payments Industry Education Program is designed to help payment professionals reach new levels of understanding into the payments industry.

Glenbrook's Payments Boot Camps® and Private Payments Workshops are comprehensive, covering industry topics from "soup to nuts." We cover business structure and economics, market positions and strategies, technology, regulation, operations, and risk management. We discuss current trends and issues and place both into the context of current industry practices.

Glenbrook Payments Industry Education

Glenbrook Payments Boot Camp

- Glenbrook's popular Payments Boot Camp is a two-day "deep dive" into the payments industry, covering the basics of the industry, current issues, and the emerging fintech landscape.
- The agenda is structured to ensure that you understand how the industry works as a whole. We cover industry fundamentals, the dynamics between stakeholders, the impact of technology, and how the industry is changing.

Private Payments Workshops

- Let us bring our experts to your team. A Private Payments Workshop gives you a unique opportunity to expand your team's knowledge of the payments industry.
- The agenda for each workshop is customized to fit the needs of your organization. We start with material from Glenbrook's flagship Payments Boot Camp and can adjust agenda topics and topics depth.

Through this unique Payments Industry Education Program, Glenbrook shares its experience and insights with payments professionals eager to understand industry fundamentals and how they are evolving.

For more information on Glenbrook's Payments Industry Education program and to see the current workshop schedule, visit our website at **www.glenbrook.com**. For information on scheduling a Private Payments Workshop, or to place bulk orders for this book, please contacts us at **bootcamp@glenbrook.com**.

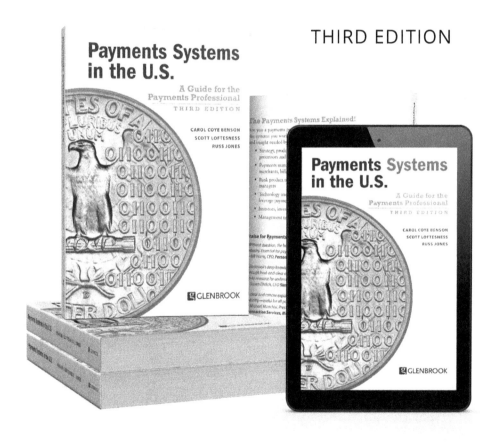

CPSIA information can be obtained
at www.ICGtesting.com
Printed in the USA
BVHW051702270421
605947BV00007B/1091